New Orleans from the foot of Canal Street

Southern Travels

The Historic New Orleans Collection
Richard Koch Publication Fund
Patricia Brady Schmit, General Editor

Southern Travels

JOURNAL OF
JOHN H. B. LATROBE
1 8 3 4

EDITED WITH AN INTRODUCTION BY
SAMUEL WILSON, JR., F.A.I.A.

PUBLISHED BY
THE HISTORIC NEW ORLEANS COLLECTION
1 9 8 6

For Ellen Elizabeth Latrobe Wilson

The original manuscript of John H. B. Latrobe's 1834 journal is among the John H. B. Latrobe Family Papers (MS. 523) in the Manuscripts Division of the Maryland Historical Society Library. This volume is published with the permission of the Maryland Historical Society.

End Papers:
New Orleans from the foot of Canal Street looking North, ca. 1834
Pencil and watercolor by John H. B. Latrobe
The Historic New Orleans Collection (1973.38)

International Standard Book Number: 0-917860-21-7
Library of Congress Catalog Card Number: 85-81188
Richard Koch Publication Fund
©1986 by the Historic New Orleans Collection
All rights reserved
First edition. 2,500 copies
Printed in the United States of America

CONTENTS

ILLUSTRATIONS

FOREWORD

The Richard Koch Publication Fund, the result of a bequest from Mr. Koch, will enable the Historic New Orleans Collection to add another dimension to its decade-old publication series. The purpose of the fund is to publish travel diaries and other early accounts of life in New Orleans.

Richard Koch, an outstanding architect who, among other achievements, was elected a regional director of the American Institute of Architects, was paticularly known for his effective restoration of historic Louisiana buildings. A dedicated preservationist, he was the district officer for Louisiana of the influential Historic American Buildings Survey during the 1930s. This work was the genesis of the Vieux Carré Survey, a monumental architectural research compilation, which is housed at the Collection.

The original journal kept by John H. B. Latrobe of his 1834 journey to New Orleans is owned by the Maryland Historical Society. We are most grateful for their permission to publish a document of such particular interest to New Orleans. The journal has been edited by Samuel Wilson, Jr., noted New Orleans architect and Mr. Koch's partner for over twenty years.

Stanton Frazar

.

PREFACE

The magic lantern, gracing the parlors of nineteenth-century America, brought the exotic and distant to life for its entranced viewers. On a wall or screen, the beam of the powerful lamp projected images of foreign scenes, taking its viewers far from the mundane and the familiar. Explorers were heroes to Americans then, and travel was their preoccupation.

For a contemporary reader, a travel journal can be a magic lantern, projecting images of a way of life that is now foreign in time, rather than place. Like Proust, the reader can find "plenty of charm in these bright projections which seem . . . to shed . . . the reflections of such ancient history." Unself-consciously, travel journals bring their times to life in vivid glimpses.

To observe intelligently, to draw comparisons and contrasts, to reach conclusions, and to express one's thoughts in clear, well-crafted prose: these were hallmarks of the civilized man in the last century, and John H. B. Latrobe, whose account of an 1834 southern journey is presented in this volume, exemplified this model. An acute and thoughtful observer, he recorded his travel impressions in pithy and vigorous language.

Latrobe's journal is a travel *cum* adventure story, a shrewd commentary on the contemporary scene, and an extraordinarily rich social history. A travel journal is a particularly appropriate representation of American life because travel itself satisfied the restlessness, gregariousness, love of novelty, and infatuation with mechanical advance that were so characteristically American.

Travel in the 1830s was an adventure, and it took a blithe spirit, not only to endure, but to enjoy the tedium, dirt, bad weather, oddly assorted companions, discomfort, sharp regional differences, and even danger. Accidents, such as the near shipwreck and the runaway stagecoach suffered by Latrobe, were not just dramatic incidents of this journey, but virtually everyday occurrences.

Democracy was the rule in American travel, and a traveler who held aloof from his fellows was resented mightily. A forced close association with strangers — often unwashed, uncouth, and bug-ridden — was an expected aspect of travel. Except in big-city hotels, innkeepers commonly expected strangers to share rooms and even beds. On shipboard, the cramped quarters and stench found in the reserved cabins sometimes induced travelers such as the Latrobes to move to cots in the general cabin.

Latrobe seems to have had an affable, easy manner and enjoyed chatting with the peddlers, slave traders, and frontier tavern keepers he encountered. As he wrote in this journal, "Your selfish, silent traveller is but a poor acquirer of knowledge . . . the traveller who looks only, and does not talk or listen carries about with him the feelings & prejudices of the only land he knows, his home, and is wholly unable to appreciate the peculiar characteristics of the new people among whom he finds himself."

Latrobe's travels offer a capsule view of American transportation. In a two-month trip, he traveled by all common modes of public transportation: under sail in a merchant ship from New York to New Orleans, upriver to Natchez and down again by steamboat, out to Lake Pontchartrain by rail, across the lake by steamer, and then across the southeastern states in a stagecoach on his return trip to Baltimore.

Graceful deepwater sailing vessels ruled sea trade and travel for years after steam had taken over the rivers. Sailing ships were cleaner, quieter, and, with good wind, much faster than steamboats. By the time Latrobe made his journey, steamboats had begun to venture onto the ocean, but it was not until after the Civil War that steam largely replaced sail on the seas.

Dirty, puffing, noisy steamboats had surpassed sailing vessels and flatboats to dominate trade and travel on America's inland waterways during the last twenty years: the first steamboat voyage on the Mississippi — commanded by Latrobe's brother-in-law in 1811 — ushered in the new era on western waters. Steamboats could make way upriver against the current and could guarantee their schedules with more accuracy than their competitors. By the 1830s steamboats were the workhorses of the rivers.

Latrobe's brief journey on the railroad running from downtown New Orleans to Lake Pontchartrain was a minor part of his journey, but mirrored a major part of his life. The 1830s were a period of railroad-building mania not equalled until after the Civil War; Latrobe was counsel for the Baltimore and Ohio, the first passenger railroad, and his considerable professional success was based on the growth of that line. At first, rail travel depended on the appeal of novelty, but by the 1830s a number of railroads were expanding their services nationally with the new iron rails and steam-powered engines. Although as dirty and noisy as steamboats, rail travel was far preferable to the alternate means of land transportation — the stagecoach.

In choosing not to return home by ship, Latrobe sentenced himself to stagecoach travel since the southern states lagged in railroad building. He chose to jolt through the backwoods of the southeast by stage, enjoying a series of odd encounters and adventures. Coaches were a teeth-rattling way to travel, sprung only by leather bands, which sometimes gave way, sending the coach body crashing. Seats were hard and narrow; when too many passengers boarded the coach, a middle third seat was pulled up to the detriment of comfort and leg room. Windows were usually covered with ragged leather curtains, so that they were drafty and dusty, and during the winter, as Latrobe found, very cold.

Country roads were abominable, knee-deep in dust in summer and in mud in winter, interspersed with sections of "corduroy," rough logs laid crosswise across the track to keep vehicles from bogging down completely. Interminable stretches of road ran through forbidding, virtually uninhabited forests. Drunken coach drivers were commonplace as they whiled away the tedious hours by applying themselves to the bottle. There were few inns or taverns along these roads, and comforts were catch-as-catch can. The wise traveler, such as Latrobe, was prepared to make his bed in the coach and to carry some provisions.

But more than merely illustrating the travails and pleasures of early travel, this journal touches on important political, economic, and social issues of American life and reflects aspects of nineteenth-century culture. Because of shared language and traditions, as well as alliances in two world wars, friendly relations between the United States and Great Britain seem in the twentieth century to be inevitable. However, Latrobe's acid comments on "the pride of the British government," and his assertion that "Great Britain manages in some way or other to give the world great trouble" reflects the suspicion of an American generation which vividly remembered the War of 1812. Britain was the premier international power, dominating world trade; until very recently American traders had been excluded from the lucrative British West Indian trade. The British had just annexed the Falkland Islands, flouting the Monroe Doctrine. Even more explosive were boundary disputes between the two nations along the Canadian border with the Oregon territory and Maine; indeed open conflict erupted in Maine later in the decade. Suspicion and restrained hostility characterized Anglo-American relations in the early nineteenth century, and another war was not considered out of the question.

Domestically, slavery was the crucial moral and social question for Americans. The 1830s opened a tumultuous period, leading to the Civil War, in which militant abolitionists denounced slavery as a sin, demanding immediate freedom for slaves, and diehard apologists for the institution argued that slavery was economically essential to the nation and that it provided the proper social order for blacks.

Latrobe opposed slavery, commenting that "the many were labouring for the one in the very worst form of servitude — negro slavery." However, he dreaded the possible consequences of abolition and sought a compromise which would avoid social and economic upheaval. In the 1820s he had joined the American Colonization Society, which numbered such prominent Americans as Henry Clay and Andrew Jackson among its members. The basic plan of colonization was to encourage the freeing of slaves, but then to transport free blacks to African colonies to avoid racial conflict. The society purchased the colony of Liberia, but colonization was never a great success, partly because most free blacks declined to emigrate.

In 1834 Latrobe was still hopeful of the ultimate success of colonization since the Maryland branch of the society had that year set up its own agricultural colony for freed blacks, Maryland in Liberia. He discussed colonization with fellow travelers and of one conversation reported optimistically that his listener thought the Maryland Plan, "would remove all objections to Colonization in the South."

Latrobe, however, believed strongly that the white and black races must always remain separate and distinct in the United States. Shocked fascination was his response to the rainbow spectrum of racial mixture he encountered in New Orleans: he devoted pages to speculation on the racial identity of the people he encountered.

For a curious gentleman touring this notoriously lax port city, attendance at a quadroon ball was almost mandatory. Latrobe, moralizing all the while, visited two. Of the young mulatto women who graced the balls in search of a protector, he said, "I pity the poor creatures whom the white man's sin makes infamous, and devotes to prostitution from their cradle." He was referring to the system of *plaçage,* in which young white men set up houses for their mulatto mistresses, often encountered at a quadroon ball, and for any children of the liaison.

The nineteenth century was an age of belief in limitless economic progress, based on technological and industrial advances, and Latrobe, whose success was securely hitched to railroads, subscribed wholeheartedly to that belief. The idea that destruction of the natural environment could be considered detrimental was far from Latrobe's mind. Indeed, for most Americans in the nineteenth century the vast forests of the nation were simply wilderness, barriers to progress. The more quickly they were cleared for farms, settlements, or industry, the better for the young, burgeoning nation.

Latrobe noted with approval every sign of economic development. On the stretch of the Mississippi from the Chalmette battleground to New Orleans he commented appreciatively on the buildings and businesses solidly lining the river bank. He pointed out several extensive brickyards, a large sawmill, an immense cotton press, and the hundreds of merchant vessels in the river and at the docks. That was progress, and he was for it.

The application of steam technology to mills and presses he found particularly interesting, often making arrangements to tour and to learn about their processes. On visiting a cotton press, he noted such details as the number of bales pressed per day and the price per bale for the service.

For a man enamored with economic progress, New Orleans was an exciting city. The hub of a world trade network, the port was the transshipment point for manufactured goods from the Northeast and Europe; for flour, grain, and other staple commodities from the Midwest; and for cotton, sugar, and tobacco from the South. It was also the busiest slave emporium in the country: a steady stream of slaves from the declining Southeast were put on the block here to satisfy the demands of the fast-growing plantation economy of the lower South.

Southern Louisiana was not suited to the predominant cotton culture, but by 1834, when over 100,000 hogsheads were produced, sugar had become the staple crop of the state. Latrobe was very interested in what, to him, was a novelty, commenting that sugar plantations presented "the most beautiful appearance that I ever saw in any species of cultivation." He took every opportunity to learn about the growth and processing of sugar cane. Fortunately,

Southern Travels

New Orleans was surrounded by a complex of sugar plantations, many of them equipped with steam-powered sugar mills employing the latest scientific advances in processing.

The dark side of booming New Orleans, though, was ill health and epidemic disease. Mortality and disease rates throughout the nation were extremely high, particularly among women — Latrobe, though a young man, had lost his first wife — but New Orleans was notoriously dangerous. The city was attacked almost every summer by yellow fever, which often rose to epidemic proportions. Pandemic Asiatic cholera had reached the shores of the United States only two years before this journal was written. The outbreak in New Orleans had been fierce, and it was feared that cholera would also reappear annually. Actually, the disease had nearly run its course by 1834 with only sporadic appearances, including the second Mrs. Latrobe's attack.

Those who could afford it left the city during the summer months, closing down their houses and business affairs, returning in the late fall when the worst dangers of disease were past. On the voyage down from New York, Latrobe observed that the "passengers are mostly persons returning to New Orleans after the sickly season to resume their respective occupations."

Latrobe himself was quite healthy, but he had a particular dread of illness in New Orleans because his father and his older brother had died in separate yellow fever epidemics there. He feared it so that he suffered an attack of acute hypochondria, imagining that he was coming down with the fever. But he said, "I determined not to be sick if I could help it in New Orleans where associations of ideas alone would have gone far to kill me." By morning, he had recovered his spirits and found that he had not, after all, contracted the dread disease.

Besides the dramatic, fatal epidemics, Americans also suffered from a variety of less serious ailments. Dyspepsia was a national curse: eating habits seemed to be designed to cause ill health. The frying pan was the cooking implement of choice, and most people ate too fast and too much of a poorly balanced diet. A typical day's fare on shipboard, as described by Latrobe, illustrates this point. Breakfast of some dozen items, including mutton chops and chickens, was followed by a mid-morning snack of a basket of apples. At noon hunger was staved off by a plentiful lunch which included soup, meats, breads, cheese, and potatoes. Dinner at 2:00 was the major meal of the day. It always featured nine or ten meats, including goose, turkey, and corned beef, as well as rice, bread, potatoes, hominy, and a few vegetables, succeeded by a lavish dessert course, and ended with cheese, nuts, and preserved. fruits. Tea followed in the evening and "another exhibition of the eating capacities of the passengers takes place." As Latrobe summed it up, "You may readily suppose that we are well fed — and truly we are so."

Though unwise eating was not yet seen as a health problem, by the 1830s overindulgence in alcohol had come under attack from the standpoints of both health and morality. In the seventeenth and eighteenth centuries, it had been commonly believed that alcohol improved strength and spirits, as well as helping to prevent disease; a daily liquor ration was often included in workmen's contracts. Early Americans had been a heavy-drinking lot: many ladies drank bumper for bumper with their mates in after-dinner toasts, and the local tavern was the neighborhood gathering place. Both the army and navy issued to the men two- to four-ounce daily rations of alcohol, usually whiskey in the army and rum in the navy. As Victorian attitudes became more prevalent, the temperance movement gained converts, and many Americans took pledges of abstinence. The army ration was abolished in 1830, to be followed within the next few years by the navy.

Grog rations had also been traditional on merchant vessels, but the temperance movement had spread to those ships as well. Latrobe's ship was one of these. As he observed, "There is no grog served out, & there seems to be no complaint on that account." Certainly, safety and efficiency improved on ships where the crew was sober.

Originally, temperance meant just that: moderation in drinking, with a preference for wines and beers to distilled spirits. Increasingly, however, temperance was coming to mean prohibition, as its advocates became convinced that any consumption of alcohol led directly to ruin. This view ultimately, but briefly, triumphed with the ratification of the eighteenth amendment in 1919.

Latrobe was the more moderate sort of temperance advocate; he drank wine, but disapproved of drunkenness. He was shocked by the number and availability of bars in New Orleans with their "beastly gratification." He also disapproved of the elegance of the appointment of some of these establishments, commenting that, "Rum and gin . . . here live in palaces and the genius of Intemperance . . . may well console herself with the taste elegance and refinement of her shrines in New Orleans."

Particularly offensive to an American Protestant — Latrobe was Episcopalian — was the sight of carefree New Orleanians imbibing on Sundays. Sabbatarianism, the proper way of keeping the Lord's day holy, was an important issue in Protestant thought. In the most fundamental denominations Sunday was devoted entirely to religious activities — churchgoing, prayer, and serious discourse. Even idle conversation was forbidden. Without going to these extremes, all American Protestants shared at least some Sabbatarian convictions, viewing business operations, travel, social events, dancing, card-playing, and secular reading with varying degrees of disapproval. "Blue laws," that is, laws forcing Sunday closing of businesses, reflect these ideas.

The Catholic Church demanded attendance at Sunday service, but saw no harm in everyday activities for the remainder of the day. Catholic New Orleans worked and played on Sundays without guilt or consciousness of sin, and Latrobe was shocked by what seemed to him pagan and irreligious behavior. He fumed, "They work on the Sabbath . . . brandy may be drunk, or bonbons sold, or bargains made, or soldiers drilled."

These comments touch on only a few of the impressions found in John H. B. Latrobe's journal. The literary habits of Latrobe and his generation created a rich legacy of information which illuminates a vanished era. The reader can picture an earlier age, appreciating its guiding ideas and prejudices, through the eyes of an intelligent and accomplished gentleman. Latrobe's journal provides a magic lantern tour of American life in 1834.

Patricia Brady Schmit

EDITORIAL METHOD

J ohn H. B. Latrobe's journal has been transcribed literally, retaining his style of spelling, capitalization, punctuation, and abbreviation. The intent in editing has been a faithful rendering of the original text. A few exceptions should be noted: dashes at the end of sentences were replaced with periods; superfluous dashes following other marks of punctuation were omitted; when a punctuation mark or capital was unclear, modern usage was followed; superscripts were dropped to the line; and clearly accidental duplications of words were silently corrected.

Latrobe's hand is generally quite clear. In those instances when a word was missing or difficult to decipher, the probable word was supplied in square brackets. If the rendering was quite conjectural, a question mark was placed within the brackets. A completely indecipherable word was represented by a question mark within square brackets.

Annotation has been kept to a minimum, to aid the reader without overshadowing the text. Brief footnotes defining obsolete or foreign words or phrases, explaining political or cultural movements, and identifying geographical locations have been supplied for clarity, but commonplace reference sources have not been cited. Basic references used include the *Dictionary of American Biography, Appleton's Cyclopedia of Biography, Webster's Third New International Dictionary* (unabridged), *New Cassell's French Dictionary, New Columbia Encyclopedia,* and genealogical and geographical sources for individual states.

In a fifty-year career as a practicing architect and an architectural historian, Samuel Wilson, Jr., has assembled extensive research files on American architecture, the fruits of his investigations in archives and libraries throughout this country and abroad. He used those files to annotate the buildings mentioned in the journal. To cite all the sources used to arrive at these architectural judgments would have been wearisome, creating a lengthy subtext which would compete with the journal itself. The following sources were used: acts of sale, building contracts, city directories, architectural drawings and specifications, inventories, wills, correspondence, diaries, journals, and contemporary newspapers. The following

Southern Travels

repositories were consulted: Bibliothèque Nationale, Archives Nationales, Archivo General de Indias, Library of Congress, National Archives, Maryland Historical Society, Orleans Parish Notarial Archives, New Orleans Public Library, Historic New Orleans Collection, Louisiana State Museum, Tulane University Library, and Loyola University Library.

ACKNOWLEDGMENTS

Most of the papers of John H. B. Latrobe, including this journal, are in the possession of the Maryland Historical Society. The cooperation of the Society in making it available for publication is greatly appreciated; the assistance of William Keller, head librarian, and Donna Ellis, manuscripts librarian, was invaluable. I am especially grateful to Dr. Edward C. Carter II, editor of the papers of Benjamin Henry Latrobe, who first made copies of the John H. B. Latrobe journals available to me and encouraged me in having them published.

A generous bequest to the Historic New Orleans Collection by my late partner Richard Koch, the distinguished New Orleans architect, was made, among other purposes, to assist in the publication of journals and diaries of early visitors to New Orleans, such as these journals and sketches of Latrobe. I am pleased to express my gratitude to the board of the Collection — to Mr. Benjamin W. Yancey, its chairman, and to its members, Mrs. William K. Christovich and Messrs. Ernest C. Villeré, G. Henry Pierson, Jr., and Francis C. Doyle. I also thank Mr. Stanton M. Frazar, director of the Collection, and members of his staff, especially Dr. Patricia B. Schmit, Mrs. Louise Hoffman, Mrs. Lynn Adams, and Mrs. Joan Sowell, who have worked so hard in preparing the manuscript for publication. It has indeed been a pleasure to work with them.

Thanks are also expressed to Mrs. Herbert G. Brown, who generously loaned two of her Latrobe sketches, and to Mr. Don Didier, who arranged for this loan. I also wish especially to thank those members of the Latrobe family who have made family portraits and papers available for publication: Mr. Ferdinand Claiborne Latrobe III, for the use of family papers in his possession; Mr. John Latrobe, for the use of his portrait of John H. B. Latrobe, his great-grandfather; Mrs. Virginia Latrobe Ruebensaal, for use of the portrait of her great-grandmother, Mrs. John H. B. Latrobe; and to my wife, Mrs. Ellen Elizabeth Latrobe Wilson, to whom this book is dedicated, for the use of the watercolor of Soldier's Retreat, the Claiborne family home near Natchez, and for all her patience, help and encouragement in all aspects of this publication.

INTRODUCTION

The Life of John H. B. Latrobe

J ohn Hazelhurst Boneval Latrobe, whose eventful life spanned
most of the nineteenth century, embodied the best qualities of
the American character — strength, vitality, and
resourcefulness. The distinguished son of a distinguished father
— the noted architect and commentator on the American scene,
Benjamin Henry Boneval Latrobe — the younger Latrobe was born
in Philadelphia on May 4, 1803. Latrobe, a penetrating and acute
observer, wrote from the vantage point of one who possessed a
sense of America's place in history. An attorney by profession,
Latrobe was also a talented painter, architect, writer, inventor, and
historian. He was acquainted with many of the important scientific,
political, artistic, and literary figures of his day, including Samuel
F. B. Morse and Edgar Allen Poe.

John H. B. Latrobe, who was the elder son of Latrobe and his
second wife Mary Elizabeth Hazelhurst, studied at Georgetown
College in Washington, D.C., and briefly at St. Mary's College in
Baltimore. In 1818 he entered the United States Military Academy
at West Point, but resigned before graduation because of his father's
death of yellow fever in New Orleans on September 3, 1820. He
felt obligated to return to Baltimore to support his mother and
younger brother and sister.

In 1821 he entered the office of his father's friend, General
Robert Goodloe Harper, as a law student. During these years of
financial hardship, Latrobe wrote a number of articles, and in 1826
he published a well-received book, *The Justices' Practice Under the
Laws of Maryland*. Latrobe's success as an attorney was assured when

The sources of information and quotations in the introduction were the Labrobe papers in
the Maryland Historical Society and Latrobe's biography, *John H. B. Latrobe and His Times,
1803-1891*, by John E. Semmes (Baltimore, 1917). The biography was based largely on
Latrobe's letters, writings, and journals, made available to the author by Latrobe's son,
Ferdinand Claiborne Latrobe, who served seven terms as mayor of Baltimore. After Mayor
Labrobe's death in 1911, the Latrobe papers held by Mr. Semmes were given to the
Maryland Historical Society.

The Maryland Historical Society holds extensive collections of Latrobe papers, including
letters, diaries, speeches, poetry, legal writing, and news clippings. In the 1960s the Society
acquired the Benjamin Latrobe letter books and sketches from Mrs. Ferdinand Latrobe II.

he was named a counsel of the Baltimore and Ohio Railroad at its incorporation in 1827, continuing in that capacity until he died in 1891. He achieved wide recognition as a leading railroad and patent lawyer.

Besides working to establish his career and to support the family, the young Latrobe took an active interest in the public issues of the day. Through his association with General Harper he became interested in African colonization and helped to found the Maryland State Colonization Society. He made a map, based on descriptions, of the country that had been purchased as a new homeland for freed American slaves. When the map was to be engraved, Latrobe and General Harper selected names to be applied to the territory. Latrobe wrote, "Several names were suggested. . . when the General said, 'The name of a free man in Latin is "Liber," cannot something be made out of that?' And after a while. . . Liberia was adopted. . . My turn came next, when I proposed Monroe, the name of the then President which. . . was softened into Monrovia; and so we went on until the baptism was completed. The engraving of the names then followed. . . on the first map of Liberia ever made. At the next meeting of the American Colonization Society the nomenclature was formally adopted."

He continued to be an active supporter of the colonization movement throughout his life. In 1853 he was elected to succeed Henry Clay as president of the American Colonization Society, a post which he held for the next thirty-seven years.

Latrobe once said that, if his father had not died, he would probably have been an architect. A few years after leaving West Point, although not an architect, he won a competition for the design of a monument to the Polish hero Kosciuszko. He received a gold medal from the Corps of Cadets in 1825 for the monument, which still stands at West Point.

Using his father's drawings, Latrobe designed the west portico and towers of the Baltimore Catholic Cathedral, made all the working drawings, and superintended the work. He also designed several monuments in Greenmount Cemetery in Baltimore, the Baltimore Cottages and the southern portico of the Belvedere at White Sulphur Springs in Virginia, the gateway at Druid Hill Park, Baltimore and other architectural works.

In 1824 John H. B. Latrobe met and fell in love with Margaret Stuart, daughter of Dr. James Stuart of Baltimore, but no engagement was possible until he had established himself professionally. In his diary of Tuesday, October 18, 1827, Latrobe wrote: "Dr. Stuart has given me his consent, and. . . I have this day plighted my faith and received hers — the greatest gift — in return." He later wrote that "my earnings of 1828 justified our marriage, which took place November 29, 1828." A son Henry, was born of this marriage, but on January 31, 1831, Latrobe's wife died. Of her he wrote, "a truer, nobler woman never lived."

Soon after the death of his wife, he made a trip to Canada, making sketches of places he visited, a practice he continued for many years. Throughout the rest of his life, he traveled in America and Europe, making watercolor sketches in a sketch pad and illustrating his journals with pencil or ink drawings. He also painted in oils and, in later years, made fine copies of the family portraits for his children.

In August 1832 he went to Virginia for his summer holiday, stopping to visit former President Madison at Montpelier and to sightsee at Charlottesville, before arriving at his destination, White Sulphur Springs. It was here that he met Charlotte Virginia Claiborne, daughter of the late General Ferdinand Leigh Claiborne and Magdalen Hutchins of Natchez, Mississippi. The lonely widower noticed that the seventeen-year-old southern lady had a "pretty face" and shortly referred to her as "the fair Miss Claiborne," writing that she was "very pretty, very sensible and very unsophisticated" and that she "was the handsomest woman at the Springs and the most admired." When the Claibornes moved on to Botetourt Springs, beginning their return journey to Natchez, young Latrobe followed. A few days later, on August 28, 1832, he proposed and was accepted. Among his sketches of the Virginia springs is a sketch of the interior of the Claiborne cottage at Botetourt Springs.

Latrobe returned to Baltimore to make preparations for his approaching marriage; on November 1, 1832, he left again by stage for Natchez. At Nashville he met the Claiborne party, including his intended bride and her brother John F. H. Claiborne with his wife, and continued on to Natchez with them. He wrote an account of this journey and of his first visit to Natchez. His impressions of the Mississippi River and of Natchez are of particular interest:

"My first impulse on finding myself in a condition to go into the streets, was to hurry to the bluff to see the Mississippi river, for as

yet I had only heard of it. Natchez is built upon a range of high
earthy cliffs, so to speak, upon the left bank of the Mississippi and
extending up and down the river for about two miles. Between the
edge of the heights and the town there is a vacant space, a part of
which is planted with China trees, and where benches have been
placed, and at the upper end of which is the lighthouse. This is
called *the* Bluff, par excellence, and to this place I hurried and saw
the Mississippi at my feet. My first impression was a decided
disappointment, and I said to the gentleman who was with me, that
I had never seen such a mere mud puddle dignified with the name
and distinction of a great river. My first thought was for the
picturesque — with the visual character of the Mississippi I did not
at the time trouble my mind. My only thought was how it would
look in a picture, how it would compare with the Chesapeake — the
Potomoc — the Hudson — the Delaware, the Susquehannah — and
I was grievously disappointed. Imagine yourself standing about two
hundred feet above the level of a river some half mile wide at the
widest part, yellow with mud, whirling along with a turbid current,
bearing upon it, here and there, a black and decayed log, bounded
on the opposite side by a continuous range of tall ungraceful cotton
trees now bare of leaves extending inland into a dense forest and
terminating the view on either side, as a sudden turn gives to the
river the appearance of a long and narrow lake . . . At the very base
of the height on which you stand is 'Natchez under the hill,' a
collection of frame buildings, at the foot of the most southern road
down the steep, consisting of stores chiefly, and continually filled
by a population of the very worst possible description — the
boatmen of the Mississippi . . . I had in my minds eye when I
approached the Mississippi, the Potomoc below the Turkey landing
— the Delaware at New Castle, — the Hudson at the Tappan Zee
— the Susquehanna at Havre de Grace. You may well imagine
therefore that I was disappointed with what, in truth, I saw at
Natchez of the Mississippi. But this was only in reference to the
picturesque. The moment you considered the moral character of this
vast river, you found it impossible to conceive the greatness of
which it would be the cause, as its own tide and its mighty
tributaries poured the wealth of the midlands that they water to the
ocean, and brought back the rich exchanges of other climes.
Natchez is a pretty town — that is to say, the situation on the bluff
is excellent, the streets run at right angles and are sufficiently wide.
The Court House is in the center of a paled green square, there are

several very good churches and many private dwellings of distinguished elegance — others again that combine the neat and picturesque with the comfortable in an eminent degree. Around these last you see galleries with venetian blinds to them — low projecting eaves, neat basements. . . So that, take it all in all, Natchez is a pretty town of its size. It is not increasing. Other towns on the river, with a richer back country, are now dividing the business which belonged, at one time, to Natchez exclusively, and Vicksburg, Little Gulph and Grand Gulph promise soon to be its successful rivals."

The Latrobe-Claiborne wedding took place on December 6, 1832, at the plantation house of the bride's mother who, after the death of General Claiborne, had married Dr. David Cooper. The ceremony at Soldier's Retreat was performed by the Reverend Pierce Connelly, rector of Trinity Episcopal Church in Natchez. Leaving on the steamboat *Lady Franklin* on December 13, the newly married couple traveled up the Mississippi and Ohio rivers, then overland to Baltimore, which they reached on January 7, 1833. Later that year, their first son, Ferdinand Claiborne Latrobe, was born.

The following year, since Mrs. Latrobe was in poor health, they decided to take a sea voyage to New Orleans and to spend the winter in Natchez, taking their infant son with them to be baptized at Trinity Church there. Latrobe kept a journal during this journey and his return trip to Baltimore which is the subject of the following pages.

When Latrobe returned to Baltimore in late 1834, his wife remained with her family at Soldier's Retreat. It was during this time that their second son, Osmun Latrobe, was born. He was named for one of Mrs. Latrobe's brothers, Osmun Claiborne, who had been named for one of his father's close friends, Col. Benajah Osmun of neighboring Windy Hill Manor. Neither Soldier's Retreat nor Windy Hill Manor still stands.

After spending the winter and spring of 1835 in Baltimore working at his legal practice, Latrobe left in June to return to Natchez for his wife and children. Going by rail to Frederick, Maryland, then by stagecoach to Pittsburgh, he took a steamboat down the Ohio and Mississippi to Natchez. Since Mrs. Latrobe was in much improved health, they departed in a few days for the return trip up the river, then to White Sulphur Springs where they remained until the end of August 1835, then returning to Baltimore.

Southern Travels

Besides his concern for public issues of the day, John H. B. Latrobe also had a lively interest in American history. He was one of the original organizers and incorporators of the Maryland Historical Society and recorded in his diary on October 23, 1835, ten years before the Society was incorporated, that "Yesterday Johnson, Donaldson and I proposed to get up a Historical Society in Maryland." From 1866 to 1871 he was a first vice president of the Society, and from 1871 until his death twenty years later, he was reelected annually as its president.

He gave lectures at meetings of the Society, several of which were published. Perhaps the most interesting and important was "First Steamboat Voyage on the Western Waters," published in 1871. This was an account of the trip of the steamboat *New Orleans* in 1811-1812 from Pittsburgh down the Ohio and Mississippi rivers to New Orleans. This early steamboat was commanded by Nicholas J. Roosevelt, who had married Latrobe's half-sister Lydia Latrobe in 1809, from both of whom Latrobe had received firsthand accounts of that historic journey.

Among his other Maryland Historical Society addresses and publications were "A Lost Chapter in the History of the Steamboat," also in 1871, and "Maryland in Liberia" in 1885. He also presided over the sesquicentennial celebration of Baltimore in 1880 and composed a lengthy ode for the occasion. He gave the principal address at the laying of the cornerstone of the present Baltimore City Hall in 1867 and at its dedication in 1875. Commemorative tributes organized by the Society after his death priased his many contributions and the high esteem in which he was held.

Throughout his life, travel was one of John H. B. Latrobe's chief pleasures. He made perhaps his most eventful journey in 1857 at the end of an extensive European tour with his son, Ferdinand. In Paris they had encountered a Baltimore acquaintance, William L. Winans, whose firm of Winans, Harrison and Winans had secured a contract with the Russian Government to remount the Nicolai Railway between St. Petersburg and Moscow. Mr. Winans first requested Latrobe, as a lawyer, to review the Russian contract; he later persuaded Latrobe for a fee of $60,000, then a considerable sum, to spend the winter in St. Petersburg as his legal counsel. Young Ferdinand Latrobe returned home while his father proceeded to Russia, recording the events of his long visit and of his meeting with members of the Russian royalty and nobility in his penetrating and thoughtful journal. The Winans's mansion in Baltimore (now demolished) was called Alexandroffsky, and their country place near Baltimore was called the Crimea, recalling this Russian adventure. The friendship between the Latrobes and the Winans family, now living in England, has continued to the present time.

A man who also placed high value on his private life, Latrobe was a devoted husband and father. The Latrobes eventually had seven children and every year on their wedding anniversary he wrote a romantic poem to his wife. On their golden anniversary, December 6, 1882, he wrote, as a fifth and closing stanza:

> And so, dear wife, thine eyes to me
> Have all their laughing brilliancy,
> As when from Southern waters
> I bore away my winsome bride,—
> The choicest gem, the joy, the pride
> Of Mississippi's daughters.

John H. B. Latrobe died in Baltimore on September 11, 1891, at the age of 88; his wife Charlotte Virginia survived him until 1902.

Latrobe, the intelligent traveler, wrote of his travels, "I have had rare travelling for a drudging lawyer. . . North, South, East and West have my wanderings been. If not wiser I am healthier; and at all events if I have found my country with all the inconveniences occasionally of almost a savage State, I have seen her in her vastness, and now know and feel the certainty of her future and inevitable grandeur and glory among the nations of the earth."

Samuel Wilson, Jr., F.A.I.A.

JOURNAL

DR. RALPH DRAUGHON, JR.

CURATOR OF MANUSCRIPTS

THE HISTORIC NEW ORLEANS COLLECTION
533 ROYAL STREET

(504) 523-4662

October 27th 1834

My dear Brother.[1]

The ship Arkansaw[2] Dennis, Master, on which for the first time I have ventured to sea, is now making her way under a fine land wind past the highlands of Neversink[3] on her voyage to New Orleans. As yet I have felt nothing of sea sickness, and take advantage of my exemption from that which has already prostrated Charlotte[4] to make a beginning in the way of journalying the events of my present expedition to the South.

Nov 2nd.

I had scarcely finished the above paragraph, before I was called to attend my wife, who after eating a hearty dinner on the smooth waters within Sandy Hook, yielded to the first swell as the vessel stretched on her course out upon the ocean. She has since been very ill, and I have been kept in constant anxiety about her. To day, when we are in Latitude 27° N. she appears to be somewhat better and I am in hopes that the smooth sailing which is promised to us on the Bahama Banks will set her upon her feet again. I too have had my full share of the disagreables of a sea voyage, and for the last two days have been moping about the very picture of woe. I was up at first and was congratulating myself with having escaped this worst of human afflictions, when I was suddenly attacked, and in the course of ten minutes felt more dead than alive. I should have been much worse than I was, had it not been necessary for me to attend to my wife; and often, after straining my eyes out over the lee taffrail, I had to rush to her assistance, and hold her head

1. Benjamin H. Latrobe, Jr. (1806-1878), an engineer for whom the city of Latrobe, Pennsylvania, was named. He began his engineering career with the Baltimore and Ohio Railroad in 1829.

2. New York coastal packet built in 1833, in service until 1850. The following advertisement for the *Arkansas*'s return voyage to New York appeared in the *Louisiana Advertiser* (November 15, 1834): "For New York — New Line. The new and splendid ship *Arkansas*, Capt. Dennis, is now ready to receive cargo and will have immediate dispatch. For freight or passage, having handsome accommodations...."

3. Navesink highlands, situated along the northeast New Jersey coast on Sandy Hook Bay.

4. Charlotte Virginia Claiborne (1815-1902), wife of John H. B. Latrobe.

over a basin, until by the time she was relieved, I was fully prepared to repeat my own scene on the quarter deck. I verily believe that the efforts I made to avoid a simultaneous discharge into the basin, did more to cure me than all the nostrums which the old voyagers on board persuaded me to take.

We are in a gallant vessel of the largest class of merchant ships. Our captain has risen to his present rank, like Newton Forster[5] through all the gradations of service; he has the reputation of a first rate seaman well acquainted with the voyage that we are now upon. He has little of the sentimentality that Maryatt has given to his hero: but is a man of few words, bluff in his appearance, and at times unpleasantly abrupt. He is a kind hearted fellow though, and plays with the children on board, and attends to the ladies with a sailor like roughness, though with real solicitude for their comfort. "Well Captain Dennis, where are we now" says a female cabin passenger. "Why all hereabouts" replies he looking round at the unbroken expanse of horizon. "But is there any danger," persists the interrogator. "None unless the wind blows hard enough —" and at last we have all by common consent agreed to refrain from questioning him; and he stands on the poop deck leaning over the spar that is lashed between the main and mizen shrouds for a railing, hour after hour, with the appearance of a man who is deeply aware of the responsibility of his situation and is using all his mental and bodily powers to discharge it. Some years ago he was shipwrecked on the Florida coast in the Kentucky,[6] a splendid vessel in the packet line which he commanded; and sometimes when I look at him on his accustomed stand, and mark his stern and thoughtful countenance, I fancy that he is thinking of the lee shore, the tempest, the shock of the mighty ship on the rocky beach, the after struggle of those who were in her, and their scant escape from a death on the inhospitable deep. I think Captain Dennis was not always the stern man he now seems when on his quarter deck, and he becomes quite interesting, rough as he is, when I place his present silent and almost morose watchfulness to the account of his memories of the past.

The Mate Mr. Miller, is a kind hearted good natured young man,

5. *Newton Forster; or The Merchant Service* by Frederick Marryat, published in 1832. Marryat's years of service in the British navy provided background for his popular novels of sea adventure.

6. Wrecked fifty miles north of Cape Florida, November 20, 1832. See p. 32 for account of the shipwreck.

who is an excellent seaman, and is evidently much confided in by his Captain. He has excellent good sense and his observations are quite original. He has a hat for every kind of weather — and one may judge what to expect from the sky and the waves by observing his headgear when the watch that he commands takes its turn upon the deck. The second mate Vincent is a thorough going *old* seaman who has attained in his present office the highest rank that he will in all probability ever enjoy. It is a terrible and yet most interesting sight to see the old man "lay out" on the weather yardarm in reefing, and sway there to and fro with the security and ease of the invalids who occupy the rocking chairs on the deck below him. He is much the oldest sailor on board, and there is a fearless grace in every thing which he does, that is unequalled. There could not be better officers than those belonging to the Arkansas, in all the essentials of seamanship, and though we might have a more polite and urbane Captain, and the mates might be dressed generally more a la mode I doubt much whether any exchange would better us.

The crew of the ship besides the officers consists of eighteen men and boys, and with one exception, a man that we have dubbed the green horn, are picked sailors. The three boys are the smartest dogs I have ever seen, and two of them, Danes, Jim' and 'Gustus are models of beauty. The ship is a temperance ship. There is no grog served out, & there seems to be no complaint on that account. The men are all uncommonly hearty and active, and in the very fatiguing and severe weather that we have had have shown no want of the fatal stimulus, to which their class has heretofore, seemed devoted.

Our passengers are mostly persons returning to New Orleans after the sickly season[7] to resume their respective occupations. So far as I have been able to discover they are shopkeepers. A very clever one is a jeweller — another is a keeper of a clothing store, another is a master builder. A rich sugar planter and his wife are on board with several young ladies under their charge. He is a pleasant well meaning gentleman, and his wife a kind hearted woman. Charlotte and myself are indebted to them for kindness.

You have now the ship and its inhabitants before you and I will

7. Period from June through October during which those who could afford it left New Orleans. The city suffered annual attacks of yellow fever, which often reached epidemic proportions; during the 1830s there were four serious outbreaks (John Duffy, ed., *The Rudolph Matas History of Medicine in Louisiana*, 2 vols., Baton Rouge, 1958-62, II:124).

go on and endeavour to bring up the lee way that has been made during my seasickness, and truancy, relying on my recollection. The pilot left us off Sandy Hook light,[8] and availing themselves of the interval between a late dinner and sunset, the passengers arranged their state rooms and made themselves at home on board. At supper not one of the thirteen ladies on board was at table, but from the contiguous berths and from the ladies cabin came sundry and numerous noises indicative of the peculiar effect of the rocking motion of a vessel upon unaccustomed stomachs. The wind was fair and with all sail set the vessel rushed out upon the ocean under the curtain of the night.

October 28.[9]

All sail still set and a favorable wind. The ladies sea sick and complaining. The Andes in sight five miles to the windward, and a schooner to leeward hull down. There are two cows with their calves and a goat on board. The cows are an order for a planter in New Orleans, and pay their passage in milk. The goat is a part of the crew, and has made many voyages. The long boat was painted green while the Arkansas lay in port, and the goat has got the same colour from constantly rubbing against it. This morning she made many attempts to gain a footing in the cabin and persevering in them too pertinaciously, she has been collared and tied with a rope yarn to the cow house. Here she assumes aristocratic airs — Takes the weather side, where she holds a footing by straddling a spare topmast that happens to be lashed there, and keeps her neighbours the calves at a respectful distance. The calves, by the way, got into the cow house, without leave, this morning and we had no milk for breakfast. In the vicinity of the cow house are long rows of coops filled with poultry of all kinds, and the long boat contains the pig pen and sheep fold. The green horn, whose name is Casey, and the boys, Jim Gustus and Dick are the grooms of the Chamber to the pigs sheep & poultry. The passengers are beginning to learn each others names, and occupations, and some approaches to familiarity have been made. As no liquors are furnished on board, cabin stores have been laid in by most of us, and to day at dinner, sundry black bottles made their appearance. It is creditable to our company that

8. Sandy Hook Lighthouse (85 feet high), built on a peninsula in northeast New Jersey in 1763 and said to be the oldest in service in the United States.

9. This entry date, which reverts to October, is apparently Latrobe's attempt to bring his journal up to date after his and his wife's seasickness.

there was but one bottle of brandy although there are thirty cabin passengers. Night fell, and on we went with flowing sails.

October 29th

On getting on deck this morning I found all sails set, but no motion in consequence. The wind came in light puffs from all quarters. The clouds were low down and black, save where streaks of light here and there indicated the presence of a brighter sky above them. The atmosphere was close and muggey, — the sea was inky, and a long heavy swell rolled sluggishly from the eastward with the whole force of the Atlantic, causing the canvass to flap in thunder as it swayed to and fro with the motion of the vessel. The Captain with his hands in his breeches pockets, his favorite attitude was pacing the poop deck, and below the sailors were kept in incessant motion as the constant alterations in the positions of the yards required their presence now at one rope and now at another. The ladies who were getting better last evening have all, like the sails, been thrown aback by this pitching motion which the calm has produced, and there is much groaning. The cows look sea sick, and the calves are completely overcome. Even the goat has a melancholy look. The Andes has got into a gleam of sunshine and shines brilliantly against the gloomy sky to the Westward. A little bird, like a wren, flew on board during the night and is flying and twittering about the rigging, as if claiming our protection against the threatened outbreak of the elements. At 10 oclock the wind settled into a stiff breeze from the Southwest and we have been lying our course, but making little headway.

October 30th

The wind has come round to a favorable quarter, and we are booming merrily along. To day a queer bird, something like a duck in the shape of its body but with a much longer neck and a bill the upper mandible of which is curved like an eagles and is very sharp, alighted on the taffrail. The Captain creeping into the boat at the stern and edging silently towards the animal seized it by the tail and received several most severe bites in which the upper bill brought the blood from his hand profusely. The advent of the Duck created quite a sensation and we all assembled on the poop deck to examine it. Someone proposed a battle; and a quarrelsome old goose was brought up from the coops amidship, and pitted against the stranger — After a few rounds the goose was fairly drubbed, and his place was supplied by a game cock who for some days past had made himself very disagreable to his neighbours, and who was confessedly too old to boil, roast or make soup of. The game cock made a desperate fight but the bill of the duck was too much for him and he turned tail and ran away. It was then voted that the duck had won his freedom, — a note was tied to him recommending him as a valiant fellow, and he was tossed to leeward — he flew for a short distance and the last we saw of him was on top of a wave, with his missive released from the string that fastened it tossing in the wind.

The steward is a Chinese and one of the most active and excellent servants I have ever seen. The cook is also a Chinese, and his cookery is very good indeed. There are two assistant stewards, colored men, who make the gentlemens beds, clean out their state rooms, wait on table and it is suspected, drink all the brandy from the private stores that they can lay their hands on. The cook has an assistant, who with a black skin has a prominent aquiline nose and all the other features of a handsome white. He is much upwards of six feet in height, wears heavy boots with his pantaloons tucked in them, and a little bit of a quaint cap. He has a good opinion of his appearance and occasionally attitudinizes in his scullionage. There is also a stewardess, a tall and very light mulatto girl; much too large for the confined limits of the cabins, and much too dirty impertinent and intrusive for her situation. She is most heartily detested by the passengers, male and female, and it has been more than once suggested to apply to the Captain to send her forward into the steerage. This is my honor.

The ladies cabin is splendidly fitted up, every part of the woodwork being either mahogany or curled maple. Its occupants are certainly not deserving of it. Mrs. Latrobe and myself who have two state rooms in it have taken up our abode in the general cabin, and sleep there at night on cots. Charlotte has been too unwell to move about, and never could have stood the fumes of the ladies cabin. There is, attached to this, a water closet of the most approved construction, supplied with water from a reservoir, which is filled every day if required by a pump which goes into the sea from the deck near the wheel, and one would suppose that such an accommodation would be constantly used, and no resort would be had to the common utensils which every bed room is supplied with. No such thing however. One of our lady passengers has three children on board, the eldest about four years old, and they all go

through certain necessary operations in their mothers stateroom —
The filthy stewardess never thinks of cleaning or emptying the
utensils until the middle of the day, and when her own personal
effluvia is added to that produced by a sweaty negro maid who
attends to the children just mentioned and the whole mixed up
with the bad smells produced by the neglect of the water closet, a
compound is produced of the most offensive kind. This is a great
pity for no expense has been spared in fitting out the ship with all
the requisites for neatness & comfort in all particulars. But enough
of this subject, into which I have been led by a fracas which has
been going on in my hearing between the stewardess and the negro
girl.

The routine of the day on board the Arkansas is always the same.
Soon after sunrise a bell rings which is the notice for the passengers
to get up. In about an hour afterwards breakfast is ready, consisting
of every delicacy that can be procured and kept on ship board. Tea,
coffee, cakes, fresh rolls of admirable bread, ham and eggs,
chickens, mutton chops, omelets, sausages, cold tongue, chipped
beef &c &c and all well cooked and served. After breakfast the
passengers, generally, assemble on the poop deck, and there crowd
into the jolly boat,[10] or lounge over the railing and smoke and chat
and doze away the time for an hour or two. The steward by this
time has placed a large basket of apples on the deck near the cabin
door, which rouses the loungers above, and a general picking
pairing and mounching of apples takes place, and fills up the time
until near twelve oclock, when the table is spread for lunch. This
consists of a large Tureen of excellent soup, pickled oysters, cold
tongue, ham, bologna sausages, biscuit bread & cheeze and roasted
potatoes. — After lunch, those who deserted the jolly boat to
partake of it return to their position, and get through the time as
well as they can until two oclock when dinner is put upon table.
This consists of geese, Turkey, chickens, ducks, mutton, pork,
corned beef, ham, tongue, cabbage, potatoes, parsnips, beets,
carrotts, hominy, rice &c &c — varying through the above list
from day to day, but always exhibiting the greatest plenty. There is
a desert of puddings pies custards &c followed by raisins, nuts,
prunes, almonds & cheeze — From dinner to tea time — the hours
lag lazily by. Tea at last is announced, and another exhibition of
the eating capacities of the passengers takes place over excellent tea
— black & green, coffee, milk, toast, bread & cold relishes of

10. Boat of medium size belonging to a ship and used for general rough or small work.

various descriptions. Nine oclock finds most of the passengers in bed — From this account you may readily suppose that we are well fed — and truly we are so. Barring wine and liquors, which are not furnished by the ship, there is nothing which can be asked for at the pantry which you may not procure there — no grumbling at trouble, no stint as to quantity — The effort of all persons connected with the ship appears to be to gratify the passengers to the utmost extent.

To day there was a proposition made to create a stock for the voyage. This is done as follows, each person who is willing to subscribe, at a dollar a share, mentions the time which he thinks the vessel will be in reaching the port of destination — and he whose estimate is the nearest, takes the capital paid in on the arrival of the ship. As the end of the voyage draws nigh, the stock holders buy and sell and speculate, and an interest is created which serves to furnish conversation and amusement for many an otherwise dull hour. The time fixed now is the passage of the bar at the mouth of the Mississippi, dating from the passage of the bar at N York which we have fixed at five oclock on the 27th October. The greater number of the stockholders have taken themselves in, for in making their estimates they took no account of the time when their period would expire, and most of them expire in the night when the ship cannot cross the bar if she would. The knowing ones on board, who avoided this mistake have laughed much at the others — and the night stock as we call it has become very unsaleable.

There is a single chess board in the ship which is pretty constantly occupied, and some half dozen novels which have been read by most of us a dozen times before, but which are now in great request. Two copies of the memoirs of Vidocq[11] are in great demand indeed. One of them belongs to me, and when I shall get it I cannot tell as my politeness will not allow me to take it from the hands of the young gentleman who studies it from morning till night, and will blind himself with its small print before he has done.

October 31.

The wind is favorable and the weather fine and the ship makes great headway. Our Captain carries all the sail he can, and the

---

11. Eugène François Vidocq (1775-1857), the principal agent of the French police, whose memoirs were published in 1828-29.

vessel being remarkably stiff bears more than I could have thought possible. The Captain I find is more approachable than I had at first supposed, and at times has his long yarn to spin for you as well as another. The more I see of him the more confidence I have in him. No one can be more watchful and attentive than he is.

November 1.

Still fine weather and favorable winds & still we go booming along over the gentle swell of the seas. The steerage passengers appear to have been very sick, but are now getting over it, and exhibit themselves upon deck forward of the main mast. There is an Englishman among them with his wife and her sister — I mention them because the *ladies* wear their hair *en papillote*[12] all day long, which somewhat strongly contrasts with their *locale* and their attire — The steerage passengers are generally respectable enough in their outward guise, and are all going to seek their fortunes in *New Orleēns* as they term it.

November 2nd

This is Sunday and one of the loveliest Sundays I ever beheld on land or water. Not a cloud is to be seen; the breeze is strong enough to carry the ship from six to eight knots an hour; and nothing can be more balmy than the atmosphere. We expect to make the Bahamas tomorrow, and of course feel nothing of the wintry winds which are in all probability sweeping over the homes that we have left. The sailors are idle about the deck — the cabin passengers are lounging as usual — and those in the steerage have collected on the platform on the forecastle with books in their hands, or grouped in quiet and orderly knots. I proposed to have prayers in honor of the day, and one of the passengers undertaking to make the responses, I read the morning service of the Church of England to a small but most attentive audience — all the cabin passengers attending and most of those belonging to the steerage. The English women had let out the papillotes, and were quite gay in their appearance. After church we had a good lunch and the day was spent pretty much as usual. Towards night a bank of clouds to the Northeast which had been following us for several days in the form of a dense mist close down on the horizon, began to rise quite rapidly and extended itself to the right and left giving out broad bright flashes of lighting at short intervals throughout its whole

12. *Trans.*: in curl papers.

extent. We took it for summer lighting, and it created no
unpleasant anticipations. The Captain, when asked what he
thought of it, shook his head. Shortly afterwards we heard him
giving orders to take in the royals. In a little while the topgallant
sails were clewed up and furled, and a reef taken in the mizen
topsail. The flying jib was hauled down, and the main course
hauled up and by the time these preparations were made the vessel
began to urge its way with visibly increasing speed and the rigging
gave forth a loud and melancholy sound, as the heavy blows of a
squall swept among it with unusual violence. In about half an hour,
the sky cleared up to the Northward, and we saw the squall
whirling a vast body of clouds and mist far before us to the
southward. We have felt its skirt only. The reef was now taken out
of the mizen topsail, the topgallant sails set, the main course let
full, and by bed time we were spanking it along under a strong
breeze and with a motion of vessel considerably increased by the
effects of the squall upon the waves.

November 3rd

I was disturbed frequently last night by the tramping of the watch
upon deck and the loud vociferations of the officers. Sail was
sometimes taken in, and then again set, and several squalls passed
by towards the Southward. Early in the morning I got up, and
found the aspect of the heavens and the sea very different from
what it was yesterday at the same hour. The clouds were very heavy
and rolled along near the surface of the water. Their hue was cold
and their edges ragged and ill-defined. To the northward there was
evidently a hard rain. The waves were much higher than I had yet
seen them and the wind was directly aft. The ship had a great deal
of canvass set, and dashed along with great velocity, rolling
excessively and most uncomfortably the while. Captain Dennis was
on deck and when I came out of the cabin was giving orders to set
the fore and main royals and the foretopmast studding sails.[13] To
my inexperienced eye there was sail enough before these additional
square yards of canvass lent their aid to propel the ship, which as
soon as she felt their influence darted forward with appalling speed,
and with less rolling than before. The wind seemed at the same
time to increase, and I saw the tops of the waves cut off by it, and
the thin spray either whirled away to leeward or borne down their

13. (Stun s'l). Light sail set at the side of a principal square sail of a vessel in free winds to
increase its speed.

20

sides in long white streaks. The Captain seemed to know his business however and by this time I had acquired so much confidence in him as to make no enquiries, fully satisfied that he was doing for the best. About breakfast time the sun came out for a few moments, and shone brightly upon the vessel. But the contrast of her illuminated sails with the stormy sea and the dark clouds, and the roaring wind was too strong to be agreable, and I almost felt glad when the driving wind dimmed its rays and finally obscured it altogether. Still we hurried on with this great press of canvass — and at breakfast drank our coffee without setting down our cups, and eat from our fingers without pretending to use such things as plates and knives and forks. The trunks under the table began to shew some disposition to change their position to the injury and inconvenience of our shins, and more than one passenger found himself against the stateroom partition when he ought to have been closely fixed to the table. After breakfast I went on deck and found the Captain as busy as a bee taking in sail — the studding sail was brought down on deck the royals and topgallant sails clewed up and furled, the spanker brailed up and the fore and main topsails double reefed. A reef was also taken in the main sail and the mizen top sail. Just as these preparations were completed and when everything was snug the squall whose approach had caused the diminution of the sail struck us with the violence of a hurricane, and carried us along with it faster than we had yet gone. Just before it made its appearance, the cry of land had been made, and we saw the island of Eleuthera, about ten miles off on the larboard beam. We were now running away from it, and steering more to the westward to make the Island of Abaco on the starboard bow. When the squall struck us we were between the two islands, somewhere; and it was the Captains expectation that it would pass over us so as to afford a sight of the hole in the wall[14] from which to take our departure for the Bahama Banks. In this expectation he was however disappointed. The wind increased in violence every moment, and the sea rolled with the whole force of the Atlantic in mountain waves. In the cabin chairs, trunks tables and passengers dashed from side to side, and the only place of safety was to be seated on the floor with your back against the bulk head and your feet against some firm object. I was on the poop

14. Natural bridge-like formation projecting from the island of Abaco. Latrobe's father, Benjamin H. B. Latrobe, made a watercolor sketch of the scene on his voyage to New Orleans in 1818.

deck during the early part of the squall, and the sight was awfully beautiful to one who witnessed it for the first time. The great ship of 630 tons was tossed by the waves as though it had been the toy boat of a schoolboy. Now a wave rolling up behind her would raise the starboard quarter high in air while the larboard side of the ship would be buried scuppers under the deep hollows of the sea. Rushing up the opposite ascent with all her spars creaking and groaning; the sea acting upon her larboard bow, together with the effort of the vessel to right herself would cause her to roll as far to starboard as she had just done in the contrary direction; and thus she staggered onward like a drunken man but with surprising speed. On coming down from the poop deck with a rope of the ladder in each hand, the weather roll took me completely off my feet and I hung suspended by my hands until the ship righting herself enabled me to regain my feet in safety. After blowing in this violent manner for about half an hour the rain began to descend in quantities which I never saw equalled, and the horizon became narrowed to the diameter of a mile beyond which the mist and rain rendered it impervious to the sight. This continued for upwards of an hour. At first thinking that it would soon clear off the Captain kept the vessel before the wind — but after a little while he gave orders to lay her to. This was done, and we quietly awaited the result of the hurricane. If the weather cleared away so as to enable the land to be seen we were in perfect safety. If on the contrary the atmosphere remained as it was our situation was a most dangerous one. With Eleuthera on one side and Abaco on the other, without being able to see either or know their exact position, there was every reason to dread being driven upon the rocks; where every soul on board would in all probability be lost. Captain Dennis though he said nothing was evidently most anxious; and there were too many on board who had made the voyage frequently, not to have us informed of the full danger of our position. Under these circumstances it may well be imagined that we remained in the cabin rather a silent set of companions and that we hailed with infinite joy the shout of the first mate from the main topmast as he announced land five miles off on the weather beam, and coming upon deck stated it to be the highlands of the Island of Abaco, near the Hole in the wall. This made every one of us at ease. The ship was again put before the wind, and away we went as fast as the hurricane could bear us directly upon our course. In an hour afterwards the rain ceased, the sky brightened, we got into smooth water, comparatively, under the lee of Abaco, and with a gale of wind bore away for the Banks. More sail was now set, and we soon overtook and passed two large brigs and a bark, and by sundown made the Berry Islands on the edge of the Banks, and took our departure for crossing the shallow waters on which we now found ourselves.

In the earlier part of the voyage I had more than once wished to see the waves run mountain high, and longed to study a storm at sea on the element itself. I have now had my wish, and feel so well satisfied with what I have seen that I have not the slightest desire ever to be again in the situation, in which I found myself this morning. A storm at sea may have, and indeed certainly has its beauties but its terrors when experienced on a lee shore and land bound far counterbalance anything of the picturesque that it may contain.

Among the accompaniments of a gale by far the most disagreable part to me is the howling of the wind among the rigging. There is a melancholy and ominous sound in it which speaks of shipwreck and death.

I forgot to mention in the foregoing notice of the gale of this morning, that in the midst of it we spied a small schooner lying to under our lee under a rag of her foresail, and pitching up and down with the most tremendous motion apparently but in fact in the greatest security. For a while we all admired it, and numerous comments were made upon the bold daring of the hardy mariners who in so tiny a craft braved the sea and the tempest. Our opinions however were very considerably changed, when we were informed that it was a wrecking schooner cruizing like an ill omened bird for prey in the channel so fruitful of shipwrecks between Eleuthera and Abaco. In fair weather the wreckers remain along shore and pursue their occupations of fishing among the keys & islands of these seas: but when the storm comes on and when the heavens are charged with destruction to the traders who are caught in these dangerous parts of the ocean, the wrecker hurries to his craft, and when no other thing can live upon the waters dances over them in safety and joy towards his anticipated prey. To him the signal gun is a note of merriment, the inverted flag[15] the harbinger of gain. The loss of life never occurs to him as a subject for grief, all he fears is that the waves may anticipate him and swallow before he reaches there the rich goods and the strong ship which he is hurrying to

15. Maritime distress signal.

seize. I allow nothing for the good that is done and the assistance that is furnished at times by the wrecker when I speak of him as an individual; for this is collateral to his main object as he considers it, and perhaps rarely if ever crosses his mind. His inducement is the salvage of forty or fifty percent that is allowed him on what he saves of the cargo; and in his direct interest to promote shipwreck rather than to prevent it. It would be bad, indeed if the wreckers abandoned their occupation. They are indeed a good and not an evil of the West Indian seas. But it would be far preferable if Government had the wrecking business in its own hands, and saved without salvage that property which now pays so large a percentage to the hawks and vultures of the waters. With the vast commerce of our country the expense would be nothing, and altho both Eleuthera and Abaco are English territory, there can be little doubt that for the purpose here indicated proper accommodations would be afforded to the vessels and stations that might be necessary.

This supposition as to the readiness of great Britain to facilitate the views of the United States is perhaps not justified by her conduct heretofore. Still however it is reasonable to suppose that it would not be refused.

The Island of Abaco on the Southern extremity of the Little Bahama Banks is the land always made by vessels sailing from any of the more northern ports of the United States to New Orleans. Vessels from New Orleans get at once into the Gulf stream and follow it along the coast of Florida and past Cape Hatteras, finding it a most efficient auxiliary in making way against the northerly winds that usually prevail. But on a voyage to the southward the Gulf stream is crossed near Cape Hatteras and the vessel escapes from its influence and urges its course on the Atlantic. As it goes to the South it generally has a favorable wind. The Islands of Eleuthera and Abaco form between them the Channel by which it finds its way into the Gulf of Mexico, and the Hole in the Wall on the latter Island is the land first made, or sometimes the navigator prefers to make the opposite coast of Eleuthera to avoid the risk of falling into a current that sweeps with great force into a bay on the northern shore of Abaco. The Hole in the Wall therefore is a most important point, and the government of the United States has applied again and again to the British government to put up a lighthouse there offering to bear half of or if necessary the whole of the expense.* The English have promised as often to

*See page 107 for a retraction of of the hard things here said.[p.89]

24

build the lighthouse at its own cost, and has refused permission to the United States to use a portion of its territory for that purpose. In the meantime shipwreck after shipwreck occurs and the wreckers are the only persons who do not lament and complain of the pride of the British government which will not permit them to suffer the work to be done by the United States and their parsimony which prevents them from doing it themselves. Now, if a vessel nears the Hole in the Wall towards evening it is obliged to lay to all night for fear of going ashore in the dark, and even then if there should happen to be, which is not infrequent, an easterly gale, its chance of escaping is always more or less precarious: whereas with a light on Abaco, smooth water might be reached at all times with perfect safety.

At sundown this evening we made the Berry Islands on the edge of the Great Bahama Banks, and passed near enough to them to see the dwellings of the British pilot station there. A government pilot lives on the Island to take vessels into New Providence, where the judiciary of the Bahamas is located. The Islands are barren in their appearance and this evening wore a singularly bleak and desolate aspect as the heavy sea produced by the morning's gale dashed an angry and lofty surf upon the rock bound shore. Some years ago the British had a station here for the suppression of the slave trade, and their cutters stopped all vessels bound across the banks to ascertain whether or not they had slaves on board. The conduct of the commanders in this preventive service soon became such as to make the whole system a perfect nuisance. They were rude and brutal often in their behavior, and took great pleasure in giving trouble to the Yankees. The station has since been abandoned, and the cutters are no longer a nuisance to the fair traders of the Bahamas seas. Great Britain manages in some way or other to give the world great trouble, and the last place that I should have expected to have heard of her would have been among these rocky islets off the coast of Florida.

As soon as we got on the Bahama Banks the waters which had before been of the deepest blue appeared of what is in my opinion a dirty green, which grew lighter and lighter until they bore the hue of dirty soapsuds. At this time we were in not more than three and an half fathoms water, going along with a powerful breeze, with all sail set, at the rate of ten miles an hour and without the least perceptible motion. The evening was a delightful one and the contrast with the terrors of the morning very strong. We sat up late

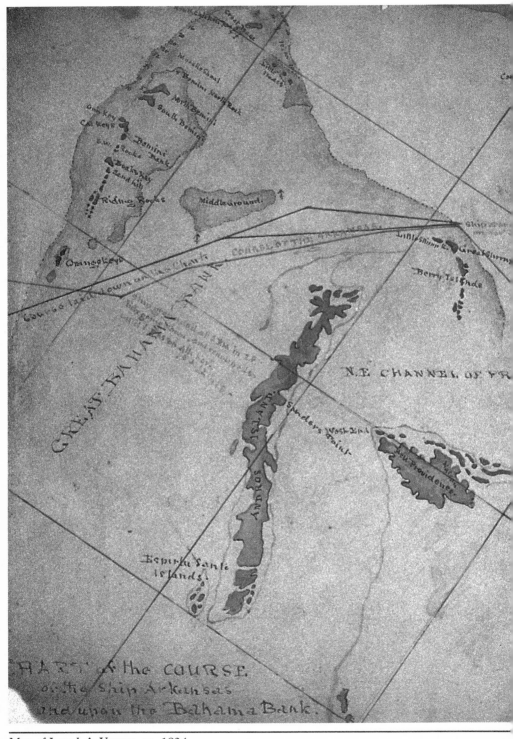

Map of Latrobe's Voyage, ca. 1834
Pen and watercolor by John H. B. Latrobe

and retired with the prospect of being again in blue water beyond the banks before daylight.

November 4th

In the middle of the night I was awoke from a sound sleep by the roar of the wind in the rigging and went upon deck. The sails were all taken in except the foresail and maintopsail, and upon asking the second mate whose watch it was how we were getting along he told me that we were fast aground. This accounted for the increased noise of the wind in the rigging; and after looking about for a little while I went quietly to bed and enjoyed a sound and undisturbed sleep for the first time since leaving New York. When the sun rose the wind did the same with a view of forcing the vessel through the sand and mud into deeper water the Captain set all sail. In a sudden squall the foretopmast studding sailboom was carried away, tearing a large hole in the foresail as it [did]. The ship did not budge an inch. After waiting till breakfast was over the main hatch was opened and the cargo moved so as to get at a quantity of paving stone which it was proposed to throw overboard to lighten the vessel. About ten ton of this was added to the difficulties already caused to the navigation of the banks when the ship gave a sudden jerk and bounced forward a few inches. All sail was now put on, and after an hours anxious suspense she began to jump ahead — and after a little while to move steadily forward through the mud large quantities of which came to the surface in her wake. By three oclock she had full way upon her, and at sundown, with the orange keys bearing west ten miles we left the Bahama Banks and found ourselves again in blue water. While aground the wind blew very strong and before we were fairly afloat the water was quite white with the sand brought up by the rolling of the waves. In fair weather the bottom is easily seen, and even the spunge which grows upon it in lage quantities. When we passed it was more opaque even than the Mississippi.

The stone thrown overboard had no effect on loosening us not having lessened the draft of the ship an inch — it was to the tide which rose two feet that we were indebted for our deliverance. It was said indeed by a wag on board that old luck was our friend on the occasion, for four of the steerage passengers had smuggled themselves into the boat astern and were quietly enjoying a game of all fours[16] at the moment that we first started from the sand. At

16. Card game.

times it is very dangerous to be aground on the Bahama Banks. When there has been a wind for a long time in the same direction, a considerable swell is raised, and the ship thumps up and down on the sand until as has been more than once known her masts have thumped through her bottom. The ship Crawford was lost in this way some years ago. As it was we escaped without any damage, and the loss of the stone which had been shipped as ballast was not of any consequence. Two of our passengers had very heavy freight on board. One of them stoves and iron, and the other a large quantity of marble for mantle pieces, and while the discharging of ballast was going on they manifested great uneasiness less their goods might be the next sacrificed to the safety of the ship. A large quantity of hats and sieves seemed to be the safest things on board as they were the lightest.

November 5th.

This morning on getting on deck I found that we had made up for our detention on the Banks by a noble run during the night. The Double headed shot keys were far behind us, and at breakfast time the light house at key west was plainly visible from the deck. At sundown we made the Tortugas and the last thing which I saw before retiring for the night was the light which marks it looking like a solitary star on the very edge of the horizon. While the British government has done so little by way of facilitating commerce in this quarter the United States have done everything, and a succession of lights lead the mariner in safety along the entire extent of the coast of Florida.

Today I found out the business of all my companions. He. is a jeweller. H.U.F. & W. are keepers of clothing stores. Two more are dry goods sellers — one is a paper seller — another is a mason & builder, another has a lot of stoves & iron there are three clerks — one boot and shoe seller — two apothecaries — one Lottery man — a planter and a watch maker. All these persons are highly respectable in their appearance and behavior, and are the best behaved set of men that I have met with for a long time. Not a game of cards has been played on board, and not a bottle of spirits drunk since we left New York.

For want of something better to do we this afternoon indited one of our fellow passengers for eating fifty clams out of the soup at lunch this morning. A jury was impanelled, and the trial proceeded, I on the bench, with all the forms of judicial proceedings.

Witnesses were summoned and after a full argument the defendant was found guilty and fined three bottles of porter, and the sheriff having suffered a witness to escape was fined as much. This furnished the afternoons [lunch?] in the cabin and relieved us from the intolerable ennui which is now beginning to set at [defiance?] eating and lounging and reading and writing.

Nov 6.

This morning we are in the Gulf of Mexico and a lovelier sky never shone above any sea, a milder and more balmy breeze never ruffled any waters in the world. The waves dance along with a merry and crisp motion — now and then curling into light and feathery whitecaps, now darkening until the deep indigo becomes almost black under the influence of the freshening wind. The flying fish are in shoals around us glittering like silver as they speed their short course in the sunlight. The sails of the native barks of oceans, the tiny Portuguese men of war, are all spread as they go by us, now bending over to the breeze like vessels of human forming, now rising up from it with the fairy elasticity of their peculiar creation. The fin of a huge shark appeared for a moment to windward, and was not seen again, as though the voracious monster forbore to intrude one thought upon a scene of such loveliness as the morning presented.

The Gulf of Mexico. Of all other waters this has ever excited in me the greatest interest. Perhaps I have wished more to see the Adriatic — but the Gulf of Mexico is wedded with my earliest memories of pleasurable enjoyment. The first school book in which I took an interest was the History of Cortez — the first campaigns I ever studied were those of that valiant soldier. Montezuma was the hero of my earliest conception, and Guatemozin[17] the martyr of the most sublime devotedness to my youthful mind. Vera Cruz for years was a spot of all others that I most wished to visit and the castle of St. Juan d'Ulloa was with me another Gibraltar. A reader from my cradle almost, nothing was fixed so firmly upon my memory as Mexico, and its history. With Pizarro I had no sympathies — but Hernando Cortez was my beau ideal of a soldier. And I was now sailing on this broad gulf. Yonder underneath that little cloud which has risen within the last five minutes, lies bravery — On this very spot once sailed the caravels of the Spanish adventurers. I

17. Guatemotzin, last Aztec emperor, usually known as Cuauhtemoc; he was hanged by Cortez in 1525.

30

could scarce believe that I was in the Gulf of Mexico, and forgot when I realized it that I was no longer the schoolboy over his story books, but the grown man with the cares of family and business pressing heavily upon him. Thou lovely expanse of waters, thou hast brought back the happy memories of boyhood, and my heart is young again as I gaze on thee!

To the Gulf of Mexico.

Here where our gallant ship now peaceful ploughs the wave
Once urged their way in slender barks a handful of the brave
Far from a distant shore they came, the red cross at the fore
And the bright and dancing waters smiled as the warrior load they bore.

There were trumpets rung their loud shrill blast upon the startled seas
And the heavy canon boomed its notes of thunder on the breeze
There were battle cries, and loud hurras sent upward to the skies
As the long low coast of Mexico first met the wanderers eyes.

Gayly the light wind bore them fast, the sun propitious shone
And the wondering natives gazed in awe as the warlike fleet came on
They deemed them gods of glorious mould, those creatures tall and white
Which swept our oceans heaving breast like midnight's pallid sprite.

They saw no people on the deck no oars upon the side
And the snow white sails to them appeared like robes of glorious pride
The red cross banner seemed a plume like that no bird e'er gave
And the drum & clarion's clangor were dread accents to the brave.

The Indian raised no spear on high as neared the boats the strand
The stranger in his panoply came all unharmed to land
In place of battle's lurid fields, the gorgeous feast was spread
And wine was poured, where human blood soon floated scores of dead.

The Indian race soon found that home the vanquished ever win
The graves dull silence closed their ears against the battles din
And the gold and silver treasures which the hills till then concealed
Brought slavery to the Mexican & the Spaniards ruin sealed.

Bright bay, full many a glorious land confines thee in their shores
Their rivers and their mountains teem with rich & golden ores

31

But there's ne'er an earthly beauty which those lands can ever grace
Like the blue and sparkling waters which they clasp in their embrace.

There's not a song of triumph that the conquerer ever sung
Like the music of thy waters when on the beach there flung.
There's not a plume or pennon that waves as fair and free
As the light and foamy white cap that dances on thy sea.

November 7th.

The day is a delightful one: but the wind has nearly died away —
and we are getting most lazily along. The Captain and I found
ourselves seated in one of the quarter boats today and I led him to
giving me an account of his shipwreck in the Kentucky.

"I would not have been lost" he said "but for a little schooner
that passed me in the night as though she were a bird in the air. I
was beating between the northern end of Abaco and the Florida
coast against a very heavy wind, and having stood as far to the
Westward as I thought proper, I wore ship and went upon the other
tack. In a little while I saw a schooner coming right down on us as
though she would jump out of water on the forecastle. She passed
close abeam, and the man at her helm shouted "You're on the
white water and will ground on the Bahama Banks." He scarce had
time to say this when the wind took him far to leeward. I thought
he was wrong but nevertheless threw the lead, and found 25
fathoms. My chart told me I was right & I stood on — but in half
an hour afterwards threw the lead again and found 25 fathoms
where according to my calculations there should have been no
bottom. Hardly supposing it possible that the Kentucky had not
gone ahead, I came to the conclusion that I was too far to the
Eastward and that the schooner man was right so I had all hands
called, and at 1/2 past one in the morning wore ship. I had hardly
done so when I saw breakers ahead on the starboard bow, and land
to leeward. It was too late to ware [wear] again for I had no room.
To anchor would have been to have perished for we should have
foundered. But one thing remained to be done so I put the vessel
before the wind and drove on to the land in the heaviest gale I was
ever out in. She grazed and slided along for some distance until a
great wave took her like a nurse takes a child and raised her high
up on its breast — and when it passed under her down she came —
the topmasts came down at the same time and her whole stern was
torn away. Every soul on board was prostrated, and the sea came

over us like the falls of Niagara. The land seemed but a short distance ahead, and we every moment [neared?] it thumping all the time with great violence. Morning came at last, and we endeavored to launch the stern boat. A smart boy got into it and just as we were letting go a wave struck it and dashed it into pieces no larger than scupper nails. We thought we had seen the last of him and gave him up for lost. But the young boy was a good swimmer and the waves helping him he got to the beach before any of us. We next cut away the railing amidships and shoved the long boat to the waters edge and launched her. The mate and three men got in but they had scarcely put off before a sea swamped her, and the next we saw was the long boat bottom upwards with the four fellows clinging fast hold to it. She got ashore and so did they. We were now in a bad plight enough. We had no boat and could not tell how long the vessel would hold together. A sailor man the best swimmer on board said he could go to shore, and he jumped in to try. He swam a dozen strokes — a big wave took him, turned him over four or five times and we saw no more of him. This only made matters look more gloomy. At last I got a couple of mattresses from the cabin, lashed a rope to them and heaved them overboard. They soon got to shore, and the mate and four sailors there hauled on by it until they got a larger rope and fastened it to a large log on the beach. We then heaved it taught [taut] with the capstain so that it was altogether out of the water. The cook, a smart active fellow said he would try it and he did so. When he got half way a sea took him and we saw no more of him. He went after the sailor man. The masts had been cut away when we grounded — but the waves tossed them about so that there was no using them — and after the loss of the cook we were in despair. At last I fastened myself to the rope and by signs made out to those ashore to haul on it: they did so and got me safe through the surf more dead than alive. The rope was then pulled back by those aboard, and by pulling it backwards and forwards we at last got every one on dry land. But it was a sorry sight to see the ship. The storm lasted three days. Then it fell calm, and we went off to the wreck and got something to eat for in the meantime we had fed on the fish thrown up by the waves. We turned the long boat upside down for a house, and lived as we could. At last the wreckers came, and on the eleventh day I got away. The mate staid to look after the wreckers — and got away in three weeks. We saved one thousand dollars worth of goods, and the wreckers got fifty percent of it. The

schooner that had misled me went on shore high and dry ten
minutes after he spoke us. The Master drank like a fish and so did
the mate. In that gale fourteen sail went ashore within one hundred
miles of Cape Carnarveral. The wreckers made more than the
underwriters did. It was sad enough for me: but I had done my duty
and saved all the lives but two. I sometimes think of it when I get
into a passion, but never without pain. I drove away like a wild
fellow for two years after I became a master — but this business
sobered me, and now I take things as I find them and try to make
the best of them."

This was the Captains story of his wreck on the coast of Florida
and was told by him much better than I have been able to write it.

I have talked much with the sailors: but find them generally
without any views of getting from before the mast. There is but one
on board who appears to have any idea of keeping ultimate
advancement in view. He is a smart young man, and tells me the
secret of the failure of young sailors is to be found in their fondness
for imitating the ways of old sailors, who as is pretty well known
are anything but models.

Captain Dennis tells me that the best officers of merchant vessels
are to [be] found among sailors from down East, particularly
Nantucket and New Bedford, where the long whaling voyages
furnish the very best school for them, and where having an interest
in the profits of the voyage they do more to preserve their
respectability than sailors whose pay is regular. The best seamen
and those most to be relied on come, he says, from the Chesapeake
Bay.

November 8th. Saturday.

We rose this morning expecting to see the lighthouses at the
mouth of the Mississippi. But we had made little way in the night
and were disappointed. A pilot however came on board at breakfast
time from a low sharp schooner to windward, and we learned from
him that we were twenty miles from the river. A strong westerly
current had carried us to the west during the night and when he
boarded us we were opposite to the southwest pass where it was our
intention to enter. The moment he came on board, after calling
out to take in the studding sails and change the course of the ship,
he went down to the pantry and asked for rum. He was a savage
looking devil and no doubt was as bad as he looked — "No rum on
board" said the second steward, "this is a temperance ship." "But

you have it for medicine," he replied "and I must get some of that
— call the steward." Henry the chinese now came. "I want some
liquor" said the pilot "Got none" said Henry — "cold water ship"
"But you have it for physic," repeated the man. "No, all cold water
ship this, no rum. Plenty cold water very good." "Damm cold
water" said the pilot as he went forward. The Captain has
permitted him to be on board but pays no attention to him further
than to take the course from him, at which I am rather glad than
otherwise for I should not like my own vessel if I had one to be put
in charge of one who evidently sought it as he would a grog shop.

The pilot had not been with us for more than an hour when the
light house at the Southwest pass[18] began to show itself above the
horizon and at the same time we saw a steamer making out towards
the ship to take her across the bar. The anxiety of the passengers
now was to know what boat they had fallen into the hands of.
Some wanted the Whale, — others the porpoise, — others the
shark, and the disappointment of all was equal when we ascertained
as the steamer drew nigh that it was the Natchez that was to tow us
up to the City — A boat proverbially slow, and decidedly the worst
in the business. She came out bouncing over the waves and
rounding too along side secured a hauser,[19] and took up her station
about fifty feet before the bow. We were now six miles only from
shore, but could see nothing of it except the light house, a few tufts
of reed and the lookout at the pilot station on the right of the
entrance. As we came nearer however a long low line of coast
became visible just rising over the edge of the water, bordered with
vast numbers of black and melancholy looking logs, some of which
were fast upon the bar and the surf dashed over them with an
impatient swell as it swept onward to the muddy banks of the pass.
Several large ships lay at anchor, and without any objects to
contrast with save the reeds assumed gigantic proportions as their
outlines were clearly marked against the bright noonday sky.

The light house is on the left side as you enter the river, and in
its neighbourhood are some sorry looking dwellings inhabited by
oystermen and fishers. The light house itself is a tall ungainly
structure with nothing ornamental in its appearance. It is

18. Originally built in 1831, the lighthouse collapsed in 1838 and was rebuilt on the west
side of the pass as a brick tower with a light at 70 feet above sea level. The tower, now
abandoned, still stands (David L. Cipra, *Lighthouses and Lightships of the Northern Gulf of
Mexico*, U.S. Coast Guard, n.d., 34-35).
19. Large rope for towing, mooring, or securing a ship.

whitewashed as also the residence of the keeper, a strong and comfortable dwelling along side of it. Some distance, perhaps a mile above the bar on the right side of the pass, a small bayou extends for a short distance at right angles with the shore, and here there is a substantial two story house with galleries around it and several other dwellings together with three look outs of frame work: the whole belonging to the pilot establishment. The revenue cutter was at anchor off this settlement; and here the tow boat left us to return for a barque from Castine, Me. which it had promised to take up the river along with us. In about an hours time it returned, with the barque, and taking us on the other side attempted to ascend the stream. But the good steamboat Natchez had overated its abilities and after several unsuccessful attempts to proceed, it found itself obliged to drop the barque and proceed with us alone. In one of these attempts we came in great danger of being cast on shore. The inefficiency of the boat which we at first so much regretted promises to turn out to our advantage, for we now advance much faster, being the only vessel in tow than we would have done with a more powerful boat, with two or more ships fastened to it.

After dinner the passengers had a meeting on the quarter deck and a card of thanks was addressed to Captain Dennis for his kindness and skill exhibited on so many occasions during the passage.

The pass at which we entered has only recently become the principal pass of the river. Formerly the Balize[20] enjoyed this distinction — But the bar has been gradually becoming more and more shallow, until now no vessel drawing more than eleven feet [of] water can pass it, and all of greater draft enter at the South west pass. Some new change may take place however, and the Balize again be used by all vessels approaching New Orleans. The river not confined by permanent banks is constantly in every part of it altering its channel.

The business of towing boats is a profitable one, and there is much competition. The Arkansas pays $380 for being taken up to the City. The tow boat is on the high pressure plan, and consists of a hull of strong but very plain construction, a horizontal engine,

---

20. Post established by the French in 1721 at the mouth of the Mississippi River. The Balize (the beacon) was principally a pilot station and occupied several different sites. In 1834 it was located on the right bank of the Southeast Pass at Balize Bayou, above the location of the original French post.

and a small cabin for the crew on the upper deck. It is an ungainly looking thing, and not being intended for passengers has little attention paid to its appearance. The first boat down the river is the first to return, and if a ship is unwilling to be taken up by it — still there is no alternative but to sail up — it being a point of honor among the commanders of the boats not to interfere with the routine of employment agreed upon among themselves.

We passed the Yazoo in the river going to New York and I put my letter on board of her to my mother.

It is now near midnight and we are going fast up the Mississippi. The night is a tranquil and lovely one. The moon makes it almost as bright as day. The sailors are sleeping upon their watch having nothing to do. The man at the helm is leaning over the taffrail — and the passengers are all around me sleeping if they can sleep while a high pressure engine is thundering at their side. I have brought up my journal to this point and now Bon Soir — tomorrow we will be in New Orleans.

November 9th Sunday

This morning we found ourselves at sunrise forty five miles below New Orleans and travelling at the rate of about four miles an hour. Soon afterwards we passed the first plantation, Johnsons[21] on the left [sic] bank: and after breakfast the vessel stopped opposite to Mr. Wedderstrand's[22] to put out his daughters who in company with Miss Smith of Baltimore were returning home from boarding school. In honor of the occasion, the Captain fired his canon, and a chair was slung on the yardarm to lower the ladies over the side. Mr. Wedderstrand and his family were ready to receive them and we had a pleasant sight of the kind congratulations of the occasion. Three miles higher up we stopped again and landed Mr. & Mrs. Packwood[23] at their plantation — Another salute was fired, the chair again fixed, and the boat sent ashore. On its return it brought us several stalks of Sugar Cane, and the passengers forthwith set to chewing it with an avidity that I could not comprehend, for to me

21. Magnolia, located on the right or west bank of the Mississippi, about a mile below West Pointe à la Hache, plantation home of William M. Johnson. He was a wealthy planter, who had been a river pilot during the Spanish and early American regimes.

22. In 1812 John C. Wederstrand purchased a plantation in Plaquemines Parish twelve leagues below New Orleans on the left or east bank, just below the plantation of Edward Livingston.

23. In 1823 Samuel Packwood purchased a plantation in Plaquemines Parish on the right bank of the river twelve leagues below New Orleans. He owned two adjacent plantations ten leagues below the city, also on the right bank of the river.

it was mawkish and insipid.

On either side of us the sugar plantations were now seen extending from the river to the marsh or swamp in the rear and presenting the most beautiful appearance that I ever saw in any species of cultivation. The green was so vivid, the foliage so dense, and the light wind waving it to and from marked it with the varying shadows that rolled after one another like waves upon a sea. It was the season for gathering in the crop, and grinding it, and Sunday as it was every man woman and child that we saw was at work at the sugar house, the unsteady puffings of which vapour from a narrow chimney with a funnel shaped aperture shewed where the steam engine was at work — and long teams of oxen drew heavy carts loaded with the newly cut cane.

The farm houses, or plantation houses rather, in this part of the world appear to have been built, all of them, after the same model. I cannot better describe them than by the annexed sketch. The climate requires all the shade that can be procured, and to obtain it the body of the building is surrounded with galleries — There are no cellars, for two feet digging brings you to water. About a hundred yards from the dwelling are the quarters of the negroes, small huts, generally comfortable in their appearance and ranged in parallel rows. Some of them presented quite a picturesque aspect with rows of china and orange trees in front of them. Above all the buildings and exhibiting by far the most imposing appearance is the sugar house surrounded with sheds. In the neighbourhood of it the plantation bell is elevated upon a tall post, and shielded from the weather by a conical Cap. Among the many plantations that I have passed and we are now within ten miles of New Orleans, I have not seen one which did not exhibit the appearance of thriving industry. The melancholy recollection however that the many were labouring for the one in the very worst form of servitude — negro slavery, destroyed the zest with which I would otherwise have enjoyed the new scene before me.

The river is filled with shipping which trust to the wind to carry them up. As there is very little of this indispensable commodity stirring today, we have passed everything that we have seen — and among the rest a schooner full of negroes — purchased no doubt where negro slavery is valueless and brought to perish in the South. A brig from New Bedford hailed us wanting to be towed round the English Turn,[24] and asked the price from the Captain of the Steamboat. The thrifty northerner thought the price too much, and stepping down from the taffrail of his vessel, he ordered the main royal to be set in a most audible voice, and made up his mind to abide the course of the wind, and trust to it for reaching New Orleans.

We came in sight of New Orleans just as we sat down to dinner: that is to say, we saw above the tops of the trees the forest of masts with pennon and signal flags fluttering among them that marked the site of this great mart of Western trade. The battle ground was to our right, exhibiting but few marks of the brilliant victory achieved there. It was green with vast fields of sugar cane, and the smoke and steam of the grinding mills arose in many places from its surface. A large tree was shewn to us as marking the spot where General Packenham fell, and a large farm house was pointed out as having been the British headquarters.[25] So eminently peaceful was its present appearance that one could scarcely believe it had ever been the field of a prolonged and mortal contest. And yet looking at it with a military eye, it was a noble plain for armies to meet upon; and I doubt me whether a battle field was ever afforded where military evolution might be so well executed with the precision of the drill ground. But the victory has had its songs of praise, and enough of it!

From the battle ground to New Orleans the shore is lined with houses and presents the appearance of a continuous street. I noticed several immense brick yards among other things. The clay is procured from the bank of the river. In some intances a coffer dam

24. Sharp, double bend in the Mississippi River below New Orleans where, in 1699, Bienville tricked an English force into turning back and leaving the river because they believed that the French were in control.

25. The Battle of New Orleans was won at Chalmette Battlefield on January 8, 1815, by American forces led by Andrew Jackson. General Sir Edward Pakenham, leader of the invading British forces, was mortally wounded in battle and removed to die under an oak tree. Conseil, the plantation house of Jacques Philippe Villeré, served as British headquarters; surrounded by a gallery, it was a simple one-story structure with a two-story wing at one end.

of stakes is built at some small distance from the shore, and the clay is taken from within it to a depth of several feet below the surface of the water. When the river rises the coffer dam is of course overflowed, and before the time when clay is wanted the alluvion deposited has been sufficient to fill it, and from this alluvion bricks are made and the coffer dam emptied to be filled again in the same manner.

We passed a large steam sawmill, and the new barracks building here by government.[26] A little further on we came to the extensive collection of buildings belonging to the catholic nuns here and called the nunnery.[27] It had a pretty sequestered look, and the irregular form of the various parts of it, the draperies hanging as shades before the arches, and the cross on the peaked pediment of the Chapel made the establishment quite picturesque. Still further on we saw the steam Cottonpress[28] — an immense range of buildings capable of containing unheard of quantities of cotton as an Orleanite informed me — and immediately above this commenced the tiers of vessels which extend for upwards of a mile along the levee. They lie, head to stream, three four and five abreast. The one nearest the shore is connected with a platform which is level with her bulwarks — with her anchor dropped. The next drops her anchor, and moors to the first, until the tier becomes at times six and seven deep. Sufficient room is left between each tier for the bowsprits of the vessels, and to facilitate the inner vessels getting out. The Law also provides that the ships which come within the corporation limits shall have their yards apeak thus, to prevent accidents from their interlocking with each other.

As we approached the town, the Captain ordered his canon to be fired, which appeared a signal for all the idlers and loungers on the

26. New Orleans Barracks, a handsome group of columned, galleried buildings, designed by Lt. Frederick Wilkinson and constructed between February 1834 and December 1835. Renamed Jackson Barracks in 1866, these buildings at the lower limits of the city are still in use by the Louisiana National Guard.

27. Third convent of the French Ursuline nuns, begun in 1823 by the architect-builders Claude Gurlie and Joseph Guillot. The buildings were destroyed after the Ursulines built their present convent on State Street and moved there in 1912. The Industrial Canal, connecting the Mississippi River with Lake Pontchartrain, was constructed on the former convent site.

28. The Levee Steam Cotton Press faced the river below the city at Press Street. Completed in 1832, a portion of the building was destroyed by fire in 1838. A view of the building is among the marginal sketches on Charles F. Zimpel's 1834 "Topographical Map of New Orleans and its Vicinity..." (THNOC 1945.13).

levee to hurry towards the lower end of the vegetable market[29] where the vessel was to be moored. There were three ships inside of us, which were crowded with people long before we came along side, and as soon as we got within jumping distance our deck was crowded with men and boys. The mate stood before the cabin door and prevented entrance there; and leaving Mrs. Latrobe I hastened into the city to procure lodgings.

Upon gaining the land once more I found myself opposite the lower end of the vegetable market, a long and imposing building supported on columns, rough cast, and forming the shape of a V, between two streets, which here intersect each other very obliquely. Immediately in front of it on the Levee, or raised mount, interposed between the river at high water and the city, a crowd of men and boys were engaged at a game of Ball — which gave rise to every species of vociferation. Among others were three Indians, their legs bare and a coarse shirt on their shoulders, which did not cover the seat of honor. A cloth apron of about eight inches deep scarcely answered to make them absolutely decent. Numbers of people were around and the whole scene was unique for Sunday afternoon. Further on I came to the meat market,[30] a building of excellent proportions formed by collonades of square piers and arches. They were busily engaged in sweeping both markets as I passed along, preparatory to being used tomorrow morning. After pursuing *La Rue de la Levée*[31] until I came to the public square[32] I

29. Open colonnaded market structure designed by city surveyor Joseph Pilié in 1822; work was completed by builder Jean Félix Pinson in December 1823. It was extensively remodeled under the Works Progress Administration in the 1930s when the row of columns along North Peters Street was removed and again remodeled in the 1970s by the French Market Corporation.

30. Oldest building in the complex known as the French Market, this arcaded building was designed in 1813 by the city surveyor Jacques Tanesse and built by Gurlie and Guillot. In a 1930s remodeling under the Works Progress Administration, a colonnade along North Peters Street and several cupolas were added to the building.

31. Now Decatur Street.

32. Laid out in the original plan of New Orleans by the French military engineer Adrien de Pauger in 1721, the central square was known as the Place d'Armes by the French, the Plaza de Armas by the Spanish, and the Public Square by the Americans. It was renamed Jackson Square in January 1851 in honor of the hero of the Battle of New Orleans.

crossed it and had before me the Cathedral,[33] the Calaboose[34] and the building in which the courts are held.[35] The cathedral is a venerable looking building, for time and climate have quite discolored the plaster with which its bricks are covered. It has a steeple, and two towers, and its general effect although it will not bear architectural criticism is good. The calaboose, & court house are on either side of it, match each other, and with the Cathedral exhibit to the Coup d'oeil quite an imposing aggregate of Law Religion and punishment. Immediately in front of the Cathedral on the levee, venders of various sorts of goods were holding open market, and shouting forth in French English and the negro patois the merits of their vendibles to the passers by, while the seven bells of the metropolitan edifice were summoning the faithful to their prayers. In all the streets around, cafés and barrooms, it would be unjust to call them grogshops, were open and in the receipt of a full and noisy custom. Rum and gin, Monongahela,[36] and Tom and Jerry[37] here live in palaces and the genius of Intemperance driven from many of her dirty altars in the streets alley & culs de sac of the northern cities, may well console herself with the taste elegance and refinement of her shrines in New Orleans. The drinking room is large — the ceiling high, a handsome lamp or chandelier hangs from the midst — a whole army of bottles, with contents of all colours line the shelves in close array all around, and the counter with its marble slab, or mahogany board, tricked off with shining brass work, and full decanters completes an arrangement for beastly gratification such as it is reserved for New Orleans to exhibit to an equal extent. But what is this in the public square. Soldiers in a gay and tasteful uniform are passing to and from, and sundry thumps

33. St. Louis Cathedral was designed by the architect Gilberto Guillemard and dedicated on Christmas Eve 1794, replacing the parish church that had burned in 1788. Benjamin Latrobe added a central tower in 1820. In 1850 the cathedral was demolished except for part of the front wall, and the present cathedral designed by J. N. B. de Pouilly was erected in its place.

34. Spanish prison, located in the rear of the Cabildo on the upper side of the cathedral. The Cabildo, designed by Guillemard, was completed in 1799. It was the City Hall, 1803-1853; housed the Supreme Court of Louisiana, 1853-1910; and is now part of the Louisiana State Museum.

35. Presbytère, designed in 1791 by Guillemard to be the rectory of the adjacent cathedral, was not completed until 1813 when the upper story was added by the architect-builders, Gurlie and Guillot. The building never served as a rectory, but was leased and then sold to the State of Louisiana as a courthouse. In 1911 it became part of the Louisiana State Museum.

36. Rye whiskey.

37. Hot, sweetened rum drink.

Ship under Sail, ca. 1834
Pen and watercolor by John H. B. Latrobe

Courtesy Mr. and Mrs. Herbert G. Brown, Clearwater, Florida

Charlotte Claiborne Latrobe
Oil on canvas by William E. West

Courtesy Virginia Latrobe Ruebensaal, Green Farms, Connecticut

John H. B. Latrobe
Oil on canvas by John H. B. Latrobe, after William E. West
Courtesy John Latrobe, Ft. Lauderdale, Florida

The mouth of the Mississippi River near the Balize, ca. 1834
Watercolor by John H. B. Latrobe

The Historic New Orleans Collection (1973.40)

On the Mississippi below N.O., ca. 1834
Watercolor by John H. B. Latrobe

The Historic New Orleans Collection (1973.39)

Catholic grave yard N.O., ca. 1834
Watercolor by John H. B. Latrobe

The Historic New Orleans Collection (1973.37)

Apple seller on the corner, ca. 1834
Watercolor by John H. B. Latrobe

The Historic New Orleans Collection (1973.36)

Soldier's Retreat
Watercolor by John H. B. Latrobe

Courtesy Ellen Elizabeth Latrobe Wilson, New Orleans, Louisiana

upon a bass drum speak martially to the ear. Oh nothing at all, sir — the weather is fine, and a volunteer company[38] is going — to church I suppose — nothing less true — they are going to have a parade and drill, which will end in taking refreshments at the *Café des Citoyens* there at the corner. "Ah well that is all is it — a pleasant time I wish them. Allons what next. Oh you need not look with such astonishment — nothing is more common, than for the billiard tables to be on constant use to day. And that shoemaker there whom you see in his shop stretching his arms so vigorously over his last, is doing what all around him are doing, work on the Sabbath." Well, not even the shoemakers idle — an industrious people this — St. Crispins[39] servants though should keep quiet for one day in the seven at all events — faith there's no romance in pulling wax ends[40] on Sunday, though brandy may be drunk, or bonbons sold, or bargains made, or soldiers drilled with something of the picturesque. "Hah — what's that. A fine figure, a beautiful foot, an ankle like an angels — an air quite distinqué, and then so strange, and characteristic — so Spanish, with that long black veil over the head" — "Allons, we will pass her. Why she's a mulatto[41] — Fie — not at all — dont let her hear you — that's a quadroon. A Quadroon! Well, I'll know better next time. Are those quadroons on high there, in the balcony that projects from that Spanish looking house with ornamented cornice and window frames and flat roof. One of them has a veil, and all that I see are darker than she we have just passed. Heavens no, they are creoles — natives, whites — Spaniards and French mixed — born in the country — very good society. No indeed they are not quadroons. You must make the distinction. Faith so I perceive — And here are more balconies, and more females, — and there sits a solitary segar smoker in one by himself — and in another, look up at it — two old ladies, quadroons — No, those are mulattos. Well be it so the two old mulattos are also smoking cigars, under that penthouse that projects from the edge of the tiled roof. But here we are at Canal

38. Militia companies regularly held drills in the public square and participated in celebrations held there.

39. Patron saint of shoemakers.

40. Threads coated with cobblers' wax used by shoemakers.

41. The nineteenth-century South employed an elaborate system of racial designations, based on degrees of racial mixture. A mulatto was a person of half white and half black ancestry, or more broadly, anyone of mixed ancestry; a quadroon was a person with one-quarter black ancestry. A Creole was white, born in America of French or Spanish ancestry.

Street and yonder is Madame Woster's[42] where you must try to get fixed for it is the genteelest place in the city to take a lady to, Sir. Bishop's[43] is the largest but he dont want ladies, and is always filled to overflowing with gentlemen.

After walking up a long paved entry from a most unprepossessing entrance I turned to the right up a light and clean staircase, and found myself in the dining room of the Establishment. Madame Woster was in the drawing room, au troisième, and to that I ascended. I found her a ladylike woman, and having obtained a promise of rooms from her I returned to the ship for Charlotte — In a little while we were comfortably settled in excellent apartments adjoining the drawing room. Some demur was made to our nurse who is colored having a bedroom where white people would be accommodated — but this difficulty was removed upon its being represented that she slept with the child — and he, being white, little fellow, he took her under his skirts and she was permitted to have the room. The shiplanding occupies the lower part of the levee and extends up past the public square — immediately opposite to which is a free wharf where country vessels are to be seen in great numbers with their awkward ill shapen hulls and weather beaten and worn sails — above these lie several tiers of small vessels such as brigs & schooners. Here however they lie with their bows to the shore, and their cable fastened to large posts set in the ground. Next is the Steam Boat landing. The boats run in as they descend the river side by side with their sterns up stream, and present a collection of stove pipes which is to be found no where else in the world. At this time there are few of any size the low water in the Ohio not permitting boats drawing much water to run. I have taken my passage in the Diana that starts tomorrow, at noon. At the steam boat landing great platforms are run out from the edge of the Levee and of the same height. When the river *"is up"* the steam boats moor to these and unload their freight with great facility. Now however the water does not reach to their base and the boats have their bows in the mud as already mentioned. Great numbers of boats are employed to bring down cotton from the plantations along the river, and it is remarkable to see how deeply they are laden. In many instances the edge of the deck is on

42. Probably Mrs. H. Wooster who kept a boarding house at 9 Canal Street in 1838.

43. Located at Camp and Common streets, this was the largest hotel in the city in 1834. On Zimpel's "Topographical Map of New Orleans and Vicinity..." published in 1834, a view of the building appears, entitled "City Hotel kept by W. Bishop, built 1831 according to plan made by Chas. F. Zimpel."

a level with the water, and the axis of the wheels are more than eighteen inches or two feet above it. The unloading is done by hand, the bale of cotton being rolled over and over on its side by two men who use each an hook like a boot puller, save that it is sharp enough to stick into the bale. Great dexterity is soon acquired, and is indeed necessary to manage the weight. Half clothed negroes with here and there a white man are the laborers employed, and are overlooked by the merchants clerks who with memorandum book in hand pass among the bales consigned to respective houses.

Last evening after tea I walked down the levee and found myself in one continued stream of people of all ages nations and colours. French was the language that principally met my ear. Sometimes Spanish and rarely English. Perhaps the French Men talked the loudest and the most while the American stalked, uncommunicatively along, and thus gave an apparent preponderance to the people of their country on the Levee. Nearly every other man had a segar in his mouth, and at several places were small tables where segars were to be purchased at the lowest sales and of the worst kinds. One of these cigar merchants was a most amusing fellow, a huge frenchman with but one leg who supported by his crutches stood under his "boutique" as he called it, and screamed his calling and boasted the value of his wares in most stentorian accents, ending a long rigmarole with, *Messieurs, amateurs, connoisseurs de toutes coleurs, venez, venez, achetez de moi:*[44] — whirring the R's with a roll of the tongue that was inimitable. Black White and Brown stopped before him, and with true french grace he dealt with all, and with a bow and a flourish offered his own lighted segar to the purchaser to begin with. Along the levee are sheds where oysters are sold at the rate of a bit for six small watery looking and most wretched things which would not be fished up in the north. Before this oyster house a fire is made of logs upon which stands a large tin kettle in which oysters are stewed and soup made for the customers, and a well worn pan, thick with its unclean accumulations of grease is put into requisition when the taste of the consumer requires the miserable devils he purposes to devour to be fried in the rank butter, or melted lard which fills a couple of kegs beside the oyster heap. I stopped at one of these places, willing to pay a bit to gratify my curiosity; and taking a fork

44. *Trans.*: Sirs, lovers (of quality), connoisseurs of every color, come, come, buy from me.

motioned to appropriate to my use one of the little plates before me. I had not time to begin, ere the french negro had dashed a dozen or twenty drops of spiced & peppered vinegar upon the contents and dredged them well from a huge black pepper box along side. I paid my bit but left the oysters to some more strong stomached fellow, and walked away apparently much to the astonishment of the man, who wondered why such a delicacy as he had prepared for me was not greedily devoured. I would rather have swallowed ten bottles of the Fiery Brass Balsam of Don Quixot.[45]

By the time I reached the meat market house in my evenings stroll along the levee, it was dark, and they were unloading the boatloads of meat from the opposite shore to be exposed in the morrow's market hours. My appetite for beef steak in New Orleans was thoroughly spoiled by what I saw. The beef itself was bad enough and dirty enough apparently but it was clean as new fallen snow compared to the devils who bore it on their bare, black, and sweaty shoulders from the rivers edge to the stalls. There were negroes who[se] clothes seemed never to have known any other washing than the gentle rains of Heaven, and who swore and cursed and vociferated in a way sufficient to turn the hind quarter on their master's truck to carrion. As soon as the beef was brought into the market it was attached to a hook and hoisted by block and tackle to the ceiling for the night.

On my return to the Boardinghouse I sat down to write up my journal, but was quickly driven under the mosquito bars, by the assaults of these pests & torments. Not being experienced in entering the bar, some fellows got in with me and my rest was disturbed in the night by their constant hum.

November 16th.

This morning I rose with the sun, and went down to the riverside to look for a steamboat for Natchez. While here I saw how the good people of New Orleans procured water. A dozen cars with hogsheads on them were standing with their wheels in the river and the horse on the land, while their drivers were filling them, with large buckets from among the filth falling from the steamboats, and trickling from the shore where the platforms furnished, day and night a most convenient privy — or public rather, for those who had no other and better place of resort for their necessities.

45. Balsam of Fierabras, which Don Quixote and Sancho Panza took as medicine, the latter with disastrous results.

The water works erected by my father[46] are in operation, and at the corners of the cross streets along the Rue de la Levee, I saw this morning the water bubbling up from the pipes into the large cast iron box around them, and running off in a rapid stream through the gutters. At every corner were crowds of negro women filling their buckets and water carts supplying themselves from a less defiled place than the margin of the river. After my fathers death these works, in an unfinished state, fell into the hands of the corporation, and the mode in which they are at present used, is much less efficient than they were capable of under a proper management.

There is a police here in uniform called the city guard. I met several of them in the market this morning in a blue cloth dress — single breasted coat with white metal buttons, and a sword fastened to a black leathern belt over the shoulders. A dowdy uniform upon a dowdy looking set of fellows.

The vegetable market is one of the best that I ever saw. The meat market except in the article of mutton is very poor. Most of the beef comes from Opelousas, and the cattle that furnish it are small. Both markets were well filled with sellers and buyers, and there were plenty of females with long black veils, some pretty enough — and others ugly and old. Numbers of old colored women in Angola shawls were seated on the pavement with vegetables for sale before them. They were picturesque enough in their gay headdresses and with their polite manners and rapid enunciation. French, in the market, as on the levee, was the language predominant in sound.

The City proper of New Orleans lies to the north of Canal Street. Mrs. Woster's is in the upper Faubourg.[47] In the City there are whole squares filled with houses built during the times of the French and Spaniards — low browed dwellings, looking as if partly

46. Benjamin Henry Latrobe was engaged in the completion of the New Orleans Waterworks at the time of his death from yellow fever on September 3, 1820. The pump house for the waterworks stood at the corner of Ursulines and Decatur (formerly Levee) streets, and water was distributed through the streets in pipes of bored cypress logs. The site was later occupied by a fish market and in 1976 was dedicated as Latrobe's Waterworks Park.

47. The original city, called the Vieux Carré or French Quarter, as laid out by the French military engineer Adrien de Pauger in 1721, extended along the river from Canal Street to Esplanade Avenue and back to Rampart Street. The Faubourg St. Mary, upriver from the Vieux Carré, extended from Canal Street to St. Joseph Street; it was laid out by the Royal Spanish Surveyor Don Carlos Laveau Trudeau in 1788. After the Louisiana Purchase in 1803, this area, now the Central Business District and Warehouse District, was settled largely by Anglo-Americans and became known as the American sector.

intended for defense with entrances through courts. You want no
guide to tell you that they are not American or English. They give
a character to the quarter in which they are that cannot be
mistaken. They abound in the picturesque and were I to remain for
a long time here nothing would give me more pleasure than to take
views down many of the streets that I have passed through today.
In the upper Faubourg the buildings are all of comparatively recent
date few of them exceeding from ten to fifteen years of age. This is
the American quarter as contradistinguished from the City proper:
though into this last the Americans are making rapid inroads, and
the granite basements & columns of the North[48] are to be seen
intermingled with the quaint and stuccoed fronts of the old Spanish
buildings.

The man who visits New Orleans must not be a poor man. He
has to pay for every thing, and that ten pieces. I will not dilate, for
I do not want to make a record of the detail of my expenditures.
Suffice it to say I never was so imposed upon in my life, and while
I was paying knew too that I was egregiously cheated. This evening,
my friend, Mr. Harrison[49] called on me for a walk and off we went
for that part of the City where the American spirit of improvement
has made the fewest alterations in the mode of building of the old
Spanish times. I found entire Squares where there has been no
innovation, without a single two story building but composed of
rows of one storied dwellings with sheds projecting from the eves
over the pavements. The windows were of the French fashion,
opening like doors, and were very frequently placed on the inside of
the wall so as to put the window seat in the street. The walls were
generally painted yellow with white pilasters on the corners, and
white facings to all the openings. The sheds just mentioned besides
giving a singular and highly picturesque appearance to the street,
answer many useful purposes. They shade the house from the sun
and shield it from the rain, and perform the same office to the foot
passenger, whom they further benefit in the unpaved street by
keeping in some measure the ground dry under his feet. The doors

48. Newton Richards was a leading granite dealer who had the material shipped to New
Orleans, mostly from Quincy, Massachusetts. He advertised his supply of granite, stating that
"Old fronts may be taken out and replaced with Granite at short notice. A partition may be
put up so that the business may be going on in the house at the same time" (*Louisiana
Courier*, December 16, 1831).

49. J. B. Harrison, an attorney with an office at 16 Exchange Place and a residence at 167
St. Charles, shared Latrobe's interest in the colonization movement.

as I passed along were generally occupied by the female part of the inmates, and these were in most cases quadroons, or French of the inferior classes; for the fashion of this quarter of New Orleans by no means corresponded with its picturesque appearance.

We went to the Catholic burying ground.[50] The tombs here are peculiar to the place. No grave could be dug of the usual depth without coming to water, and to obviate this difficulty in the sepulture of the dead, the coffin is laid upon the surface of the ground, and a strong structure of brick built around it. This is then plastered and white washed. In some there are several bodies, and in others only one. On one side of the Yard there is a range of Catacombs, like the cells in a honey comb, in which the coffin is placed, and the mouth closed with the stone containing the inscription. I was informed that these cells were purchased for various lengths of time — Varying from one to ten years, and some were owned in perpetuity. When the lease expired, the tenant was removed, when the feelings of his relatives could not be shocked by the idea of his being inundated instead of buried as Col. Hamilton says all the people here are, and the premises were then ready for a new comer. One of the cells was open this evening.

We passed by the French Theatre,[51] a large and extensive range of buildings, containing also the City assembly room. At the further extremity of it is the house in which the quadroon balls are held — and the ticket to both being the same price, the holder of the ticket to the white ball when tired goes out and exchanges with someone who has been among the ladies of mixed blood, and who gives his ticket to get into the crowd where the taint is moral and not physical.

From the Theatre went we to the French coffee house or as the

50. St. Louis Cemetery I, established in 1788, still exists, though somewhat reduced in size. Latrobe's father and his half-brother were both buried in the Protestant section of this cemetery, much of which was sold off as building lots when Tremé Street was cut through the cemetery. The location of their graves is unknown; a stone commemorative tablet was placed in a wall of the cemetery in 1985 by Latrobe descendants.

51. Orleans Theatre, on Orleans near Bourbon, originally designed in 1806 by Jean Hyacinthe Laclotte. Work began in 1810 under the direction of architect Arsène Lacarrière Latour and was completed in 1814. The theater appears in one of the marginal drawings on the Jacques Tanesse map of 1816. On September 28, 1816, fire destroyed the theater, the adjacent Orleans Ballroom, and the entire block of buildings across Orleans Street. Both the ballroom and the theater were rebuilt; the theater burned again in the 1860s and was replaced by the Catholic Convent of the Holy Family. A hotel now occupies the site. The ballroom still stands, serving as the lobby and dining room for the hotel.

sign over the door proclaims it to be the New Exchange.[52] It is a very large room with two columns in the centre aiding to support the ceiling. From this last are suspended four splendid chandeliers that make a blaze of light in the apartment. Around the walls are the usual notices of an exchange, sales, arrivals departures, &c, &c. A large portrait of Napoleon of full size in oil is on one side of the apartment with General Washington for his vis a vis on the other.[53] Here as elsewhere there is a bar, or counter, where the usual refreshments are to be obtained. The Coffee house has always a crowd of frequenters who lounge and get and relate the news, and comprising people from every quarter of the globe who are here gathered together in the commercial bustle of a great mart.

From the coffee house I went to a gaming house. It was early in the evening and play had not yet commenced with any spirit. Some keen fellows however had set too quite early, and I saw the roulette wheel in its rapid motion, and the faro table with its patent fraud preventing card box. In one house alone I counted six billiard tables all occupied, and mostly with young men, evidently not natives, who were thus acquiring a knowledge never contemplated by the quiet dominies of the New England free schools where they received the education they were sent to make available in the acquisition of wealth in the unhealthy regions of the South. After looking in for a while at the gamblers, I returned to the boarding house, with a much better idea of New Orleans, morally and geographically than I thought I could have obtained in so short a period. It is certainly a place after its own fashion. The number of gambling houses in New Orleans is very great and they are countenanced by law. As if half ashamed of the patronage that is afforded to them, the ordinance of the corporation provides that

52. Constructed at the corner of St. Louis and Chartres streets in 1810 by Gurlie and Guillot, the building was leased to various tenants, including Pierre Maspero when it became known as Maspero's Exchange. In 1834 John Hewlett operated the Exchange Coffee House at this location, which included gambling and billiard rooms upstairs. The building was demolished and replaced in 1838 by the Improvement Bank designed by J. N. B. and J. I. de Pouilly, architects, as part of the St. Louis Hotel which occupied the entire block along St. Louis Street. The rotunda of the hotel replaced the Exchange Coffee House as the city's principal exchange and business center. The site of the hotel and the earlier exchange is now occupied by a hotel.

53. Probably the same portraits which hung in Maspero's Exchange. The Probate Court inventory of Maspero's belongings, dated October 1, 1822, listed "One large picture of Washington, valued at twenty dollars" and "one large picture of Napoleon valued at fifty dollars" (Louisiana Division, New Orleans Public Library). The artist Edmund Brewster had advertised in the *Louisiana Gazette* (April 8, 1819) that his full-length portrait of Washington could be seen at Maspero's Coffee House.

they shall not have a door opening upon the street into the gaming rooms; and there could not have been furnished a better sign to the passerby than this condition, intended to save appearance, affords. As you pass along the *Rue de Chartres* you see houses with wide and open doors, within which there is a board partition forming a vestibule of perhaps six or seven feet wide. In this partition is the door proper of the gaming house. The clink of dollars is another sign here of the proximity of one of these hells, and it is a sound which in the quiet of the night when gaming most flourishes, you hear, at every few steps along the principal street of the City. The keepers a[re] generally Frenchmen who sit at the tables with a silence that is never broken and a gravity that would become the monks of La Trappe.[54] During carnival the gamblers are most numerous, and then is the harvest of the gaming houses.

November 11th. Tuesday.

This morning I got up at daylight, and after dressing myself started upon a walk into the upper faubourg. I had the sight of the sun rising on the opposite shore of the Mississippi,[55] through a dense mist that seemed to contain in its shadowy folds a whole army of pestilences. The character of the upper faubourg is decidedly American, and wants all the picturesque effect of the city proper where the marks left by the Spaniards are still plainly visible. It is most rapidly improving and large blocks of buildings are rising in all directions. At the upper end I found an immense cotton press,[56] the buildings of which have a front on the river of upwards of six hundred feet: From a very intelligent French gentleman whom I met I learned many particulars that were new to me. The cotton when it is brought from the planter is placed between two large beams, the upper of which is made to move up and down upon heavy screws, worked by steam power. These beams press the cotton in one third less size, and while they remain closed the ropes which have been previously untied, are again fastened, the pressure is taken off and the bale is fit for exportation. The article being light in proportion to its bulk it is at once evident

54. Trappist monks, a reform branch of the Cistercians, who followed a rule of silence.
55. The Mississippi River flows almost due north at this point. The so-called west bank of the river is actually to the east of an observer in the Faubourg St. Mary.
56. Designed by Charles F. Zimpel, the Orleans Cotton Press was erected in 1833 on Front and Terpsichore streets, as projected by Charles F. Zimpel, architect. A view of the building appears on Zimpel's "Topographical Map of New Orleans and its Vicinity..." of 1834. The huge building was destroyed by fire in 1844.

how much is saved in the shipping of it by this process, two ships carrying as much pressed cotton, as three could carry in the shape in which it comes from the plantation. It takes about five minutes to press a bale of cotton, and the charge for doing it is seventy five cents. The present establishment is capable of pressing seven hundred bales a day. But a small portion of the buildings are occupied by the four presses and their two steam engines; the rest is devoted to the storage of the cotton before and after it is pressed.

When the cotton press here mentioned was built in 1832 it stood upon the edge of the Mississippi. It is now distant at least three hundred feet, so rapid is the formation here of the batture. Sixteen years ago, the gentleman already mentioned informed me the site of the press was occupied by the bed of the river whose western bank was then to be found where there are now wide streets and squares covered with buildings.[57] This change is constantly going on. One side of the river is undermined and falls in as the current rushes against it, while the other receives a slow but certain increase from the alluvion which is annually deposited there, so that while the general course of the stream is sensibly changed, the parallelism of its banks remains unaltered. While the batture is forming in the upper faubourg and upper part of the City, the river is working away the bank in the lower part and along the lower faubourg, and it yet remains to be seen what the effect will be upon the port, and the present improvement.

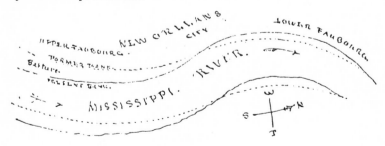

The above diagram will sufficiently illustrate the subject though

57. Soon after the American acquisition of New Orleans in 1803, a long and involved legal controversy arose over the ownership of the land added to the Faubourg St. Mary as the river's course shifted. See James A. Padgett, ed., "Some Documents Relating to the Batture Controversy in New Orleans," *Louisiana Historical Quarterly* 23 (July 1940), 679-732; and George Dargo, *Jefferson's Louisiana: Politics and the Clash of Legal Traditions*, (Cambridge, Mass., 1975), 74-101.

as it is drawn without any map or reference before me I do no pretence to answer for its geographical, or rather topographical correctness.

After breakfast I took my sketch book under my arm and walked through the old parts of the City to East of the Rue des Remparts. I again found my way to the Catholic burying ground, and seating myself on a tombstone made the sketch, page 5 of this years sketch book.[58] While seated there one of my fellow passengers in the Arkansas, a stone cutter by profession came into the yard, and prowled for sometime among the tombs. His only remark when I asked him what he thought of the spot, was, that there was not a single head stone in it.[59] His mind was runnning upon the ghostly ornaments which for generations it has been the fashion to stick up at the head of a grave, so as to render a churchyard, in the moonlight, look like a collection of the beings in their winding sheets who slept quietly beneath its surface. The stone cutter has done at all times far more to render the burial places of our race objects of terror to the living than any operations connected with the change from the moving and sentient body to the dull clod of the valley.

The Catholic graveyard wore this morning a melancholy appearance. The day was unusually warm for the season and the sky was covered with ragged and scattered clouds and the atmosphere loaded with an almost palpable miasma,[60] through which the sun shone dimly and with a sickly beam. Besides the mementos of decay that the tombs furnished of themselves, there were hanging about them faded garlands, and withered bouquets of green leaves and flowers, which on "All saints day," that has just passed, had been placed there by the pious affection of those, who in this ceremonial of the country testified their remembrance of departed relatives or friends.[61] There were marks too, in long lines of smoke upon the white plaister, where candles had been stuck at the same time against the sides of the tombs. The flowers had decayed and the

58. The pyramidal Varney tomb in the center of the sketch is now just inside the Basin Street entrance to the cemetery. See plate in illustration section.

59. Burials traditionally have been in above-ground tombs because of the high water level in the ground and because of Latin burial customs.

60. Graves were formerly believed to exude a vaporous exhalation, miasma, which contained disease-causing particles.

61. It is still the custom in New Orleans to decorate graves with flowers on All Saints Day, November 1.

candles had burnt out & the traces which they left spoke as audibly as the graves themselves of the uncertainty of the tenure of mortality. There were great numbers too of small green lizards darting in and out of the crevices in the mason work caused by the precarious foundation on which it rested, and whole rows of earthen chimneys marked the residence of the crawfish, at all times an unpleasant sight but rendered almost loathsome by its close neighborhood to the bodies of the dead. I made my sketch and left the grave yard with sad feelings, and longed for the time of my departure.

On my way back to the boarding house I paused again and again among the quaint old buildings of which I have already said so much, and do truly believe that New Orleans is as thoroughly impressed upon my mind as it is upon the minds of nine tenths of its inhabitants. Nor do I say this for the sake of the period or without a voucher: for in speaking to residents of what I had seen and hunted up I much oftener gave information, than elicited it: So true is it that what one may see every day, it is ten to one if he ever sees at all.

Having had my baggage taken down to the steam boat, I embarked at 12 O'clock the hour appointed for her departure. Punctuality is not a virtue among the river boats, and it was 2 O'clock before we set off up the river. We had not proceeded more than two miles before we stopped at a sugar plantation[62] to take on forty hogsheads of sugar. I was not sorry for this as it gave an opportunity of learning something of the manufacture of this article. I went ashore and found the manager a very polite Frenchman who explained to me the whole process, and accompanied me through the establishment. As you may be as ignorant as I was, I will repeat to you what I learned.

To begin. The cane grows from cuttings — rather from the old stalk. One third of the crop is saved for seed, if I may use the expression. Several furrows are turned in towards each other so as to form a bed. In the middle of this another furrow is run as deep as the plough will go. In this last, the stalks of the cane are laid by twos and sometimes by threes. Where the stalk is not sufficiently straight it is cut into smaller pieces. The stalks are then covered by means of the plough. This planting lasts for two years, the second years growth being called rattoon cane. Planters rarely rely

62. Probably the De Gruy plantation, then located on the west bank of the river opposite Napoleon Avenue.

exclusively on the second growth but keep planting annually so as to have the average crop from the first and second years planting about the same. When the cane reaches its proper size which is about the beginning of November it is cut near the ground. The leaves are stripped off and the thick part of the stalk is put into the mill, which presses all the juice from it into troughs leading to the Boilers. These in the sugar house that I saw, were five in number. The first is called the grand, the last the battery and the middle one the *sirop*. The grand is the lowest, and each boiler rises about two inches, so as to make the battery the highest. These five boilers are placed in a line quite close to each other and over a furnace. The juice of the cane passes from the mill into the *grand*

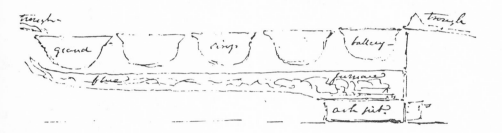

by a proper trough. Here it is a nasty looking fluid. Lime is added to it and it technically "purges itself." The scum that rises to the surface is thrown off and it is ladled into the next kettle — and the grand is "charged" again. After a certain time it passes into the 3d. kettle — then into the fourth — then into the fifth, from which when it has boiled sufficiently it is ladled into a trough which conducts it to the vats or receptacles where it cools and granulates. From there it is put into hogsheads with holes in the bottom and placed over large troughs. The molasses now runs through into the troughs, — from which it is drawn off for use — and the sugar becomes what we find it at the grocers. It will be seen that the battery is immediately over the fire, it boils furiously — the next boils less so — the next less, and so on decreasing until the last, at the end of the flue, only simmers. This is essential to the effect to be produced — and is managed in the above simple and efficient way. Some dozen negroes were busy when I was in the house, at the mill, ladling the syrup, or carrying way the sugar to the hogsheads. They were merry enough at their toil, and were in good condition and well clothed. This is the general process that I have described: of course there are many details which on so short a visit I had not time to be informed of or to understand. The mill that I have drawn in my sketch book is one of the old fashioned ones, and I should judge from its appearance that it had been erected some fifty or sixty years ago.[63] It was originally intended for horse power in grinding the cane. Steam has been introduced now, and the buildings put up since are very different in their appearance from the one which I have drawn.

While engaged in making my sketch, I saw several things that were new to me. The first was a gig drawn by two horses abreast; the second being attached to a surcingle tree extending across the shafts near the dash board. The next was a most handsome barouche in which rode a white planter looking portly and well to do in the world, with his mulatto wife or mistress, a mulatto friend of hers and his mulatto children. Truly the state of society here is miserable enough: though I am informed that as the American resident population increases there is a change going on for the better.

It took us upwards of two hours to load the sugar, and at sundown we commenced our journey in good earnest. While lying at the plantation, the Le Flore, the Boonslick, and the Juniata passed us on their way up, and two boats loaded with cotton went down. There are but few passengers on the Diana, and Charlotte and myself have exclusive possession of the ladies cabin. This is comfortable enough and makes us bear without complaint many inconveniences. The Captain is quite a clever man, proud of the speed of his boat, which is certainly great and quite a dandy in his dress. He is a little worried that he has no more passengers on board, and now has no chance of increasing them on the way, for there are three boats ahead which will intercept the way passengers that he would have had, had he continued ahead of them as when he left New Orleans.

Wednesday November 12th

We stopped at two O'clock last night in a dense fog and did not

63. The sketch, which is too faint to reproduce, shows a circular, domed sugar mill once fairly common in Louisiana, although none is known to exist today. It may have been the same mill described by C. C. Robin in his 1807 *Voyages dans l'intérieur de la Louisiane . . .* (abridged trans., New Orleans, 1966) after visiting the plantation of "a Creole named De Gruise."

get underway until sunrise. We are now getting along pretty well.

At about 11 oclock we passed the Bayou Plaquemines a very small and ill looking settlement on the East Bank of the river. Here one cabin and two deck passengers came on board. One of the latter was quite an oddity. He had been to New Orleans among the french and his conversation was taken up with abuse of them. "They gave me bread" said he, "so tough that when I stuck my knife into it, it squeaked like a piece of well seasoned sole leather, and as to their meat, if you put a bit no bigger than a pea into your mouth and *chewed* on it, it swells so much as to keep your jaws from shutting again." We wooded soon after leaving Plaquemine, and reached Baton Rouge at 2 o'clock. This village occupies the first ground not naturally subject to inundation above New Orleans. To call it a hill would be to apply a great name to a very little thing. It is rising ground on which are scattered a good many houses, none of them at all prepossessing in their appearance, and some bearing marks of a Spanish origin. As we approached the village it presented a singular appearance. The front row of houses on the river had all porches to them, and in front of these canvass was hung from the eves to the ground as a shield against the morning sun. In this way the buildings were concealed and in their stead was a long line of snow white drapery.

At the upper extremity of Baton rouge is the United States arsenal and garrison. The Barracks[64] are two stories high, well and comfortably built of brick, with wide collonades on each front. They occupy four sides of a pentagon, the fifth being open to the river. In the centre was the flag staff on which was waving as we passed the national flag, far above the surrounding tree tops, a strange, but not the less gratifying sight here in the bosom of the woods and by the deep waters of the Mississippi. There were neither steamers nor flat boats at Baton Rouge and the only sign of business which was visible was a large steam sawmill hard at work upon the edge of the river below the town. Baton Rouge is unhealthy at certain seasons, as well as New Orleans.

I had a great desire to see "the Coast"[65] as it is termed, that is

64. The buildings, now called the Pentagon, still stand in Baton Rouge near the State Capitol, built by the War Department between 1819 and 1822 as quarters for an infantry regiment. The buildings are now the property of the State of Louisiana.

65. Generally referred to as the German Coast or the Côte des Allemands, extending on both sides of the river from St. Charles Parish about twenty miles above New Orleans to Donaldsonville. The area was largely settled by Germans induced by John Law's Company of the Indies to settle in Louisiana about 1720.

the borders of the Mississippi between Donaldsonville and New Orleans, but we passed it in the night, and I lost the fine plantations of sugar with which it is closely studded. As I intend returning home by New Orleans & Mobile, I shall have another opportunity, which I trust I may not be deprived of by a night passage or a Mississippi fog.

It is now near nine oclock P.M. and we have just passed Bayou Sarah, which I saw imperfectly by the moonlight. I understand it is a thriving village, but cannot confirm the statement by my own observations.

At sundown we wooded at the point below Prophets Island, the half way mark between New Orleans and Natchez. The wood cutters' establishment was miserable enough in its appearance to justify anything that Mrs. Trollope[66] might say of such abodes on the Mississippi. I was surprised to see a hand organ on the ground before it; and looking about discovered the owner of it, a weather beaten Italian who, with his "music box" as the sailors called it strapped on his back, had ground his way up the Missouri to Galena, sometimes on foot, and then helped on by the steam boats, and was now footing it back to New Orleans. He had only been a year in the country, and complained much of the small number of votaries of the joyous science. He seemed timid and alarmed when the deck passengers cracked their rough jokes upon him, and he declined playing under pretence that the box was out of order — though I doubted him when he made this assertion. The boat shakes so abominably as my writing indicates that I must stop. I don't know what is the matter but it shakes far worse now than it did at starting. Perhaps it is that the Juniata is just behind us and we are urging our way faster than usual.

Thursday, November 13th.

Another foggy night obliged the Captain to fasten the boat to the shore at an early hour, and we are just released from our confinement.

Shreeve is without doubt the hero of the Mississippi.[67] Old Shreeve as he is called by the boatmen. He extracts a snag as my

66. Frances Trollope, English novelist and travel writer, whose *Domestic Manners of the Americans* (London, 1832) contained highly unflattering observations of her trip up the Mississippi.

67. Henry Miller Shreve (1785-1851), inventor and steamboat executive, cleared the Mississippi and Red rivers in 1830 of log jams that impeded navigation. Shreveport, Louisiana, is named for him.

friend Barnes of Boston would extract a tooth, and with the greater benefit as the relief extends not to one individual only, but to the thousands who navigate these waters. I have just been talking with a flat boatman returning from New Orleans where he left his patroon dying of yellow fever. His account of the good done by Shreve ought to be sufficient by itself to induce the largest appropriations for the improvement of the navigation of this river and its tributaries. Much that was told me by this man was entirely new. Not only does the river make constant changes in its course by cutting off bends and adding to one bank at the expense of the opposite one, but serious fears are entertained by some that its mouth will be altered and New Orleans be no longer a city of its shores.[68] When passing Plaquemine I had observed a large framework on the bank, composed of heavy timber and part of it buried in the earth. I now learned that this was placed there to prevent the river forming a new outlet there into the Gulf of Mexico and if a new outlet is ever formed over a shorter distance than the present route pursued by the stream, the descent being greater, (for the point of starting & the Gulf of Mexico will be of the same level) there can be little doubt that the main current of the river will pursue the new direction, and the old bed will become a succession of long narrow lakes, not unlike Lake Providence and Lake Washington which have been formed precisely in the manner here indicated. In this event what will become of New Orleans. Without a trade to compensate in the gain that it affords for the risk of life in remaining there — more unhealthy on the banks of a stagnant pool than on the shore of a mighty and rushing river — far from the site of commerce, it will be deserted in the moment of its pride, and be like a strong man struck by death in the fullness of health and enjoyment, a far more melancholy spectacle than if death had come only as the termination of a slow and gradual decay and protracted suffering.

But little danger is to be apprehended from the outbreak of the river at Plaquemine. There is another place which is represented to be of more importance however — the Atchafalaya bayou, below the mouth of Red River. The course of the Mississippi has been already changed at the latter place by a cutting off that has left the Red River to empty into a lake where was formerly the bed of the

68. The possibility of a change in the course of the Mississippi River, especially through the Atchafalaya, is still considered. Elaborate controls, constructed and maintained by the U.S. Army Corps of Engineers, exist to prevent such a change.

principal stream. The Atchafalaya, empties into the Gulf of Mexico, and it is thought that if the raft which now impedes it should be removed its current will acquire a [whirly?] that will draw to it the waters of the Red River, and that the Mississippi, pursuing a portion of its old course around the upper portion of the bend will

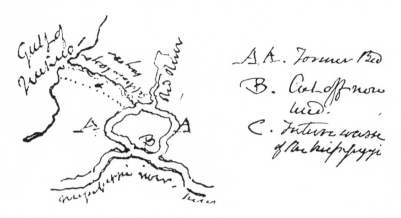

take the same direction. The adjoining sketch though wholly incorrect in the topography will explain my meaning. A great number of steam boats on their way down have passed us since we started, and last evening we had quite an alarm for a few minutes. We were on the East bank going up, at dusk, when we saw a large boat coming directly to us head on. The Captain of the Diana was afraid to change his course, lest the boat coming down which ought to have been in the middle of the stream should undertake to do the same where collision would have been inevitable so all he did was to slow his own engine and ring his bell violently. The down river boat took no notice at first and the Captain of our boat directed the pilot to run closer into the shore to be ready for accidents, when the other boat sheered off fortunately for us to the West, and we severally pursued our respective courses. The rule established by custom is that the boat going up the river has the privilege of the shore and the descending boat must keep the centre of the stream. This is in accordance with good sense, for the slack water and eddies which afford so much aid to the ascending boat are to be found under the shore, and the swiftest current is in the centre. The rule is generally well observed and the number of accidents which occur from boats coming in contact arises from the necessity of the boat going up stream crossing from point to point to avail itself of the eddies and slack water, and thus meeting the descending boat in midway. Distances on the river are very deceiving and frequent accidents have occurred from the confidence of the pilot going up that he could cross the bows of the descending boat in time, which could have been avoided had he patiently waited until the passing had taken place.

We stopped to take on a deck passenger today, and soon after passed Fort Adams, a very poor looking place with but one comfortable looking house in it, situated at the foot of the Fort Adams Hills which are the second high lands met with after leaving New Orleans, Baton rouge being the first. The Fort Adams Hills do not vie exactly with the Himalayas, but they are *hills*, and ant hills are of note in this region on unvarying level. The dividing line between the states of Mississippi and Louisiana is upon the most southern of them.

We are now within twenty miles of Natchez, in the neighborhood of which as you know, my journey terminates for the present, and I shall have now to close my journal to lock the trunks and get all things in readiness for landing.

At ten oclock we saw the lighthouse of Natchez[69] on the high bluff on the right and below it the lights glimmering in that sink of

69. The sum of $1500 was appropriated in 1826 for the erection of this lighthouse. Several 1830 sketches by Charles A. LeSueur of the completed lighthouse are reproduced in *Views of Old Natchez* (Shreveport, 1969) by James Register.

infamy and mud, the lower town.[70] How I got my family on shore is to me a wonder even at this time when we are safe on *terra firma*. The river is, as I have already remarked, very low, and there had been a heavy rain which rendered the steep Bank as slippery as glass. In addition to which a load of whiskey had been laid on the bank so as to leave a path of only three feet wide around the barrels through the mud on the steepest part as I have represented in the annexed sketch. A good natured young man took my child, the nurse scrambled along as well as she could, and I helped Charlotte up to the store house represented in the sketch. I then returned to my luggage and straddled a trunk until one by one they were carried to the store. We then got into a carryall and were dragged up the steep ascent to the upper town, where we took up our quarters at the Mississippi Hotel,[71] and furnished an admirable supper to the musquitoes who but for our arrival must have gone supperless to bed. I was in hopes that once upon shore I would have escaped these torments of a Southern life to which I had been almost sacrificed on Board the Diana, where my little boy had his face bitten upon every practicable portion of its surface — but I was mistaken, — the bars had been taken down to be washed & we were left to our fate. In the morning we moved out to Soldiers Retreat,[72] and were made supremely comfortable, by all that affection joined to unbounded hospitality could devise for us.

Friday Nov 14th.

When the Superior's boilers burst for the second time, the Engineer was seen staggering over the wheel house to the cabin where the master and the passengers were collected. "I am a dead man" he exclaimed "but there was water enough in the boilers, and it was no fault of mine." He expired in an hour afterwards. There was something striking in this incident — The man had more than ordinary force of character who in the agonies of death, thus endeavoured to vindicate his professional reputation. His skull would have been of value to the phrenologists.[73]

70. The Natchez steamboat landing was located below the Natchez bluff and was referred to as Natchez-Under-the-Hill. The site of the original town of Natchez, it later became notorious for its gambling dens and brothels.

71. Opened by William Parker in 1830 and patronized by important figures such as Henry Clay.

72. The Claiborne plantation, Mrs. Latrobe's family home.

73. Those who studied the conformation of the skull as indicative of mental faculties and traits of character.

The proprietor of the mud at which the steam Boats land their passengers and cargo at Natchez, exacts a wharfage which was evaded by the Captain of the Diana under favor of the night. The collector came on board and demanded it, and the Captain, pretending not to know him, said he was not satisfied of his authority in the matter. The agent offered to take the other to many respectable persons who would identify him, but the Captain said he was busy & could not go, and the persons must be brought to him. This of course could not be done at a late hour, and the wharf man became importunate, and the captain vociferous and abusive, ending every one of numerous long paragraphs of oaths with the assurance to the agent that he did not know him from a side of sole leather, and the threat that he would pitch him over the wrong side of the boat unless he retreated. All this occupied time, and the Captain kept it up until the passengers and cargo to be landed were out of his vessel, and then shouting "All aboard" and ringing his bell he drove off his persecutor, who with his hand in his empty pockets stood on the Bank and took out his wharfage in damming the Diana as a pickyune[74] concern and a thorough take in.

This is the end nearly of the cotton picking time in this country and the roads are crowded with wagons drawn by from three to ten yoke of oxen, conveying the bales to market. A late ride this evening brought me upon quite a picturesque group on the skirt of a tall dark wood, where a smooth green spot was snugly sheltered, hard by a deep and rugged bayou which added the attraction of a small stream of water to the soft grassy turf. Three wagons had stopped here to "camp out" for the night, and a right good supply of rails from my mother in laws[75] fence furnished a bright ruddy fire which crackled merrily, and glared into the recesses of the wood bringing the boles of the innermost trees into prominent relief. The wagons were disposed so as to form a sort of barricade and the oxen stood ruminating in the intervals between them chewing the cud in their philosophic way, or else the more substantial corn fodder that was placed before them for their evening's meal. The negro drivers were busy around the blaze and sent forth long loud peals of that hearty laughter which no one but a negro can utter, and which it does the heart of a melancholy man good to hear. There is the

74. Of little value; derived from *picayune*, a Spanish coin worth about five cents, formerly current in Louisiana and other southern states.

75. Magdalene Hutchins (1777-1852), married first to General Ferdinand Leigh Claiborne and afterwards to Dr. David Cooper. She resided at Soldier's Retreat until her death.

music of careless joy in it. It speaks forgetfulness of servitude and all
its sorrows, oblivion of the past, and the fullest and most unalloyed
conciousness of present gratification. The negroes laugh! Why it
almost reconciles one at the instant to the negroe's slavery.

There is a negro preacher in this neighborhood — bishop Punch
— daddy Punch — or uncle Punch — he answers to all names, but
prefers the first. On one occasion it became necessary in order to
fill out his discourse that he should describe the joys of Paradise.
Now as Daddy Punch had never been there he found this somewhat
of a difficult matter — but as the thing had to be done he put a
bold face on it, and said — My brethren — nigger tongue can't tell
all the joy you'll have thar' — but this much I can say You'll all eat
off golden table cloths, and have for every dinner — Roasted goose
— baked possum sweet potatoes & punkin pie" — finishing with
the proper drawl and twang. An old negress who was by could not
contain herself on hearing this annunciation of sublime joys, and
starting up, clapped her hands and shouted "God bless that sweet
mouth, jist say that thar once again." Bishop Punch is in high
repute, and is looked upon as *almost* inspired. The only scandal that
he is known to commit is that when he marries persons of color he
is pertinacious in using the Church service, and persists in spelling
all the words of their syllables, distinctly, while the couple are on
their feet before him. Never mind Daddy Punch, theres many a red
capped Cardinal whose chances I would not exchange for, were I
Daddy Punch an epicurean in opossums in Paradise, and a speller of
polysyllables.

Nov. 26.

I have had much [worry?] in the last ten days. My wife has been
attacked with Asiatic Cholera,[76] and has been preserved to me
through the blessings of that kind providence whose many mercies I
have had so often to acknowledge.

There was a severe frost last night, and the landscape looked this
morning as though it were covered with a light snow. The leaves
are falling from the trees in thousands in consequence, and make a
melancholy rustling as they fall. There is not a breath of wind
stirring. The sun shines brightly on the variegated foliage of these
huge forest trees, and the air has a crisp and invigorating tone. It is

76. A worldwide epidemic, the first cases of Asiatic cholera appeared in the United States
in 1832. Thousands contracted the disease during the next year, but by 1834 there were only
scattered cases reported (Duffy, II:139-43).

such a time as this that makes one acknowledge the truth of the beautiful and poetical name that we give to this season, when we term it the *"Fall of the year."*

I have been "possum hunting" twice. The first time I set out with a lanthorn, three negroes, four dogs and a friend and we sat in the woods on an old log from seven until eight o'clock without any barking of the dogs announcing that game was at hand. Having got chilled through we returned home — the only event worthy of recording being my alarm when a screech owl uttering its *vile* semihuman tones close at my ear made me start most hurriedly on one side to the infinite amusement of my sable companions.

On the second nights hunt we had better luck and got an opossum — though it was on the open field, and not as I deemed "up a gum tree." This time I got bewildered in a cane brake — with four or five canes under each arm, astraddle of as many more, and a [sapple?] jack twisted round my neck and hat, while my lanthorn which I held in one hand showed my situation to my companions who with no regard to my colour or my dignity roared out most vociferously at "my fix". I got fixed in this manner in trying to get out of the way of two of the dogs who were fighting and rolled by me, and appearing in my eyes to be twenty racoons in a bunch with a dog in the middle caused me to take the lateral jump that had nearly impaled me. I was exhausted when the negroes stopped laughing and soon afterwards reached home. There are sports in the world preferable to possum hunting and meats, I speak from actual knowledge, better than baked possum, daddy Punch to the contrary notwithstanding.

On my first campaign against the 'Possums I was shewn, by the light of my lanthorn an immense poplar which the winds of the last winter had prostrated, and which now lay stretched at full length in the forest surrounded with the shattered fragments of its own limbs broken in its fall and the rifted bodies and branches of the smaller growth that it had borne along with it. No inapt representation of a politician and his parasites, when the wave of party commotion has done that for the leader which the blasts of Heaven effected for the giant poplar, and his obsequious sycophants who rejoiced and grew in his shadow are overthrown by his prostration.

The trunk of this tree was hollow, and the rays of the candle were reflected along a dark perspective of some fifty feet, as we held it opposite the large hole that appeared among the roots. In the chamber there formed in the course of many winters a negro slave secreted himself some half dozen years ago, and made it his home for upwards of eighteen months. During this time he completely reversed his ordinary mode of life, never once shewing abroad in the daylight, and going forth only when darkness enabled him to plunder with impunity the poultry yards and pigstyes which he relied upon for provisions. Then he cooked in his hole, the smoke escaping unnoticed through a crevice high up among the branches and thick foliage. He was at last given up by his owner, and ceased to be thought of. The negro however became weary of his solitude. Slave as he was he could not divest himself of his local attachments. He loved the inanimate things around him too well to leave them forever, and he preferred passing the life that he did, deprived of all communication with mankind by his own voluntary act, than seeking the society of his fellows among other habitations, under other skies, where other flowers bloomed and other trees cast their shadows, than those to which from infancy he had been accustomed. He passed two winters in his den and during the second became rheumatic, so much so that he determined not to risk a third in the same damp residence. Nothing was easier than for him to have escaped; but that would have been leaving home — so one day he appeared in rags before his master, told him the history of his concealment, and again became a slave.

I have often mentioned the subject of slavery in these memoranda. I would not have you think however that I am one of those fanatics who would, if possible procure immediate abolition throughout the land. I detest and abhor the institution — but I think that it is one recognized by the laws, which can only be interfered with by the masters consent: I think too that it is a subject for the consideration of each slaveholding state by itself, and that no other state, nor the general government has a right to interfere. This principle of separate state action on the subject, if carried out will remove all objections now existing to the system of colonization,[77] and it may then be successfully prosecuted.

So far as my observation went of the slaves in Mississippi they were happy and well treated. Ill treatment no doubt was sometimes the lot of the slave. But I believe instances of it are rare.

---

77. The American Colonization Society, organized in 1816, proposed to transport free Negroes from the United States and to settle them in Africa. By 1860 more than 11,000 Negroes had been settled in Liberia. See P. J. Staudenraus, *The African Colonization Movement, 1816-1865*, (New York, 1961).

November 27th. Wednesday.

Today my second son was baptized by the Reverend Mr. Conolly,[78] the same gentleman who two years since performed the marriage ceremony for his parents. I have called him Ferdinand after my wife's father, General Ferdinand L. Claiborne. I am busy making my preparations for commencing my journey home by way of New Orleans, Mobile, Augusta & Charleston.

November 28th.

I was up betimes this morning and reached Natchez by 8 oclock. I took my passage on board the Ellen Douglass and embarked for the third time on the waters of the Mississippi. The Ellen Douglass is a large boat trading between New Orleans and Natchez and is now loaded to the gunwale with Cotton. The greatest number of bales that she has ever carried has been 1856 — but the cotton is heavier at this season than later in the year and she has now but 1756 on board. She is decidedly the best boat that I have yet travelled on in this country, either on my present or my former visit.

Eighteen miles below Natchez we stopped at Mr. Hutchins[79] my wife's maternal uncle to take in a quantity of cotton that was piled on the bank waiting for a conveyance to New Orleans. I availed myself of the opportunity to call on Mr. Hutchins and while the boat laid along shore, had much interesting conversation with him. He is an amiable and intelligent man of upwards of sixty years of age, and was the first white male who was born within the limits of the state. He has been successively under the French, Spanish, English and American rule, and has experienced all the perilous vicissitudes of a new settler in a new country. His father emigrated from Carolina to the Banks of the Mississippi, and located himself near the village of White Apple one of the principal chiefs of the Natchez tribes of Indians. For several years the number of white people in the neighborhood did not exceed thirteen, and there was around them at least a thousand Indians to a white man. After the birth of Mr. Hutchins in 1774 the country still remained very thinly settled, and it is interesting to hear him speak of the times

78. Pierce Connelly, rector of Trinity Episcopal Church. Dr. Connelly's resignation as rector of Trinity Church was accepted in September 1835. He and his wife Cornelia joined the Roman Catholic Church, she becoming a nun and foundress of the Order of the Holy Child Jesus.

79. John Hutchins (1776-1853), son of Anthony and Anne White Hutchins.

during and after the revolution. New Orleans was then a paltry village, Natchez had no existence, and the upper Mississippi was considered as a howling wilderness peopled by savages who would not permit any intercourse with the Atlantic seaboard, or the country about the Alleghenies in that direction. The only flour which could be procured came from France nicely put up in water tight casks lined with paper; and was sold readily at $25.00 per bbl.[80] Tea was $12 per lb: coffee and sugar 75 cts — salt $8 per bbl and other things in proportion. Freight from New Orleans was in those days at the rate of $5 per bbl., and the length of the voyage up was from 30 to 40 days. Everything was scarce excepting venison & wild turkies to say nothing of bear's meat. There was food for everybody provided they were content with these — beyond them nothing could be obtained except at chance seasons and at exorbitant prices. But little land was cleared, and Indian corn was not yet planted to any extent. Even this common grain was a rarity and a luxury. The fields had to be watched day & night as the ears approached perfection to preserve them from the depredations of the Indians, who took with no affectation of secrecy whatever they could lay their hands on of this new production. Even when the settler succeeded in gathering the young ears and boiling them for his table, if an Indian was seen approaching during the meal, the dish was hastily secreted, for the savage knew no ceremony, practiced no politeness, and helped himself unbidden at the board the weak hands around which dared not to provoke his anger by refusal.

The war which raged from 1776 to 1783 gave rise to no hostilities on the Bank of the lower Mississippi and excepting a single incident peace the most profound prevailed during the entire period in this remote region.

One bright spring morning while my informant Mr. Hutchins was still an infant, the unaccustomed sound of a horn was heard in the recesses of the forest near the White Apple Village, and soon afterwards a troop of white men, mounted on sorry horses, and clothed in various guise, but well armed with sword and rifle were seen urging their way along the narrow path until they emerged into the little clearing around the dwelling and outhouses. The father of the family was away, and his wife and two children with a number of negroes which last constituted his wealth & made him a rich man were left without their usual protector. Mrs. Hutchins

80. Abbreviation for barrel.

more astonished than alarmed at first by the coming of the strangers spoke to their leader in terms of kindness and courtesy and tendered to him food for himself and his companions. She was answered by loud denunciations, in which her husband was charged with being a British subject and liable in person and property to the Americans. The rude and ruffian troop yelled their approbation, and in the name of the American Congress proceeded to make themselves masters of the valuables they could find, and particularly the slaves who were at once placed in strict confinement. Nothing was spared that could be carried off. Much was destroyed whose bulk prevented it from being turned to account, and after some hours stay the troop rode off, having reduced Mr. Hutchins to poverty and passing through all the settlements in the same way vanished as suddenly as they had appeared. This it is true is but the oft told story of a border foray committed by the land pirates of the period who plundered indiscriminately on either side under the flag that suited them best at the moment, and which it cost them no scruples of conscience, and subjected them to no punishment to assume — nor should I have told the tale here but for the sequel which follows. Ten years after the robbery just narrated Mrs. Hutchins was accosted in the streets of New Orleans by a man dressed in rags and bearing every mark of wretchedness sickness and poverty. He held out his hat for alms, like a common begger, and told some incoherent story of distress. His strongly marked features caused her at once to recognize him as Willing,[81] the border plunderer, and she accosted him by name. She would have given him alms in silence, but she could not, and as she dropped the money in his hat, she told him it came from the same hand from which he had forced the silver spoons that she had prayed him to leave as a relic of her family ten years before near the White Apple village. She repented her words when she saw the shame and confusion of the humbled outlaw, who thus received good for evil, when he probably least expected it. Before she returned home she learned that he had perished in the streets. His family is still in existence and holds a most respectable rank in one of the Northern states.

From Mr. Hutchins I learned the story, authentically of the destruction of the Natchez Tribe of Indians. I had heard it before related but forgot the details, and I now give Mr. Hutchins

81. James Willing of Philadelphia raided Natchez on February 19, 1779. His ruthless tactics on this expedition turned many of the inhabitants of Natchez against the American cause.

narrative who had it from his father in whose life time it took place, and who got the particulars from the Indians themselves.

When the French were in possession of the high lands now called Ellis cliffs, and the bluff at the present site of Natchez he made an acquaintance with the Chief of the White Apple village, which was situated about six miles from the former place and some distance from the banks of the river. He was a kind old man and well disposed to the whites, and had great influence in the Natchez tribe of Indians to which he belonged. He had a daughter, a warm hearted and beautiful girl who became attached to a French officer who was stationed at the Cliffs, and as the story runs he returned her affection. For some time the French and Indians lived in great harmony; but at last the French cast longing eyes upon some fifty or sixty acres of cleared land — then a rarity in the country — around the village of White Apple their old Indian friend. They wanted it to raise corn upon for their cavalry, and they told White Apple that they must have it. This was in the early part of summer. The chief replied that it was not a fair time to ask for it — that the corn was still too young to be gathered, that his people depended upon the crop for bread, and that they could not give it up: but that if their French brothers would wait for a moon until it was secured, the Indians would move to another place and yield up the fields as they were required to do — and so there would be peace between the two people. This was certainly generous enough on the part of the Indians; but the French were not satisfied and they took the fields by force and drove the Indians away before they had gathered in their corn.

A great council was now held among the Natchez the Cherokees, Choctaws and Chickasaws, at which it was determined to attack the French and utterly destroy them. The time was agreed when the Tribes were to assemble and to ensure punctuality at the appointed day, a bundle of rods was given to the chief of each, one of which was to be drawn out every evening, and when the last was drawn the tribe was to set out on the following morning for the rendevous. The council then seperated.

The daughter of White Apple had not been admitted to the debates of the warriors, but her father assigned to her the task of drawing the rods, one by one, after explaining the object in doing so. She at once hurried to her lover, and told him of the conspiracy and entreated him to be upon his guard and to warn his friends of their danger. He treated the information carelessly and his brother officers, when they received it, laughed at and disregarded it. Day after day went by and the bundle of rods proportionally diminished and still the Indian girl saw no preparations for defence on the part of the strangers. In vain she urged her lover; and at last she became satisfied that the French were too confident of their safety to take any steps to insure it. She then determined to draw out two of the rods, so as to hasten the attack of the Natchez tribe by a single day, in the hopes that they would be defeated, while at the same time the French would be sufficiently alarmed by it to make those preparations which her warnings had failed to produce. As she anticipated, so it was. When the bundle of the Natchez tribe was emptied, the warriors began their march, and finding no one at the rendevous made up their minds that their friends had deserted them, and finding the opportunity propitious attacked the French by night, and massacred them all.[82] The next day the other tribes punctual to their appointment as certified by their bundles which no fond woman had falsified marched to the French position and found the Natchez Indians exulting in their victory and boasting that they had singlehanded achieved it. The quarrel that ensued was fatal to the victors who received at the hands of their friends and allies the fate which they had just inflicted on the French. They were destroyed nearly to a man. Their identity as a nation was forever destroyed, and while the Cherokee and Choctaw & the Chickasaw still elect their chiefs and number their warriors and sit around their council fire, the Natchez live only in the history of their destruction and in the name of the City which has arisen on the spot where their nationality was forever extinguished.

I have seen many Choctaw Indians on this journey prowling about New Orleans and Natchez. Two years since I saw the tribe on its way to Mississippi's other side. The individuals I now meet with are those who have been to their new home and returned. They are generally displeased with it, and are wandering off in various directions. Many persons think that in a few years the tribe will be extinct, and its members dispersed among other tribes or living about the settlements of the whites, finding an early death, the result of intemperance & misconduct.

November 29th.

We did not leave Mr. Hutchins until after dark yesterday. This day has been a dismal one. We have but few passengers and they

82. November 29, 1729.

are uninteresting enough. We managed to get up a game of whist this morning which helped us through a couple of hours — the rest of the time I spent reading Beckfords Italy[83] and lounging in my berth. I miss my wife very much. God bless and protect her and my little boy.

Beckford's book has much beautiful writing in it and a vast deal of extravagance, and whole pages of prose run mad. He must have been a wonderful fellow however & the publication of his letters, with the avowal that they had been read in MS by the literati of the day has exposed many a plagiarism.

While seated round the stove in the cabin this evening the conversation turned on the character and exploits of a certain John Smith now a resident of St. Louis. The name that he bore not being a very distinctive appellation he added the letter T. to it, from being a native of Tennessee, and is now known in the Country as John Smith. T. His celebrity is based upon his having killed not less than fourteen of his fellow beings either in duels or violent rencontres. He is hated and feared and travels armed to the teeth both for attack and defense. The following facts were related of him this evening by a gentleman who received them from himself.

In the early part of his life he quarreled with a gentleman named Haines. The consequence was a challenge and Haines was shot. His friends determined to avenge his death and pursued Smith into Illinois, where being joined by some fellows of his set he made a stand and in the battle that took place, himself killed two of his opponents, and defeated the party. Not satisfied with what he had done he followed them on their return home, and dispatched another by shooting him with a pistol. Four men having now fallen by his hand he became a subject of conversation, popular prejudice turned against him, and with a view of fighting himself through it, as it would seem, he had many quarrels, and having challenged a gentleman of Louisville, killed him on the island opposite the town — He now went to Illinois, and having grossly insulted an old gentleman named Brown, his son challenged Smith, and was shot through the arm and body by the monster. His next victims were two brothers named Sanders whom he fought with, selon les regles,[84] and killed one after the other. A shoemaker in St. Louis

---

83. *Italy: with Sketches of Spain and Portugal by the Author of 'Vathek'* by William Beckford. His most famous novel was the gothic romance *The Castle of Otranto*.

84. *Trans.*: according to the rules.

having as he supposed insulted him, he fired at the man in his shop and completed his ninth murder. His tenth was the result of a feud with a person whom he met unexpectedly in the high road — both drew their pistols, but Smith's alone took effect. The particulars of the three next assassinations my informant did not recollect, no wonder that he should be confused in his memory of the bloody details of crime with which this man is loaded. The fourteenth murder and it was a deliberate and coldblooded one — took place near Kingston in Tennessee. A colored man named Morgan, a light mulatto had been well educated by his reputed father, who had been brought up to mercantile pursuits, and at a proper age established as a dealer in Kingston. Here, in a wild out of the way place, at the foot of the Cumberland Mountains he met with and married a Miss Brown a remote connection of Smiths. Smith hearing of it prepared his rifle and travelled to Kingston, where he laid in wait on the outskirts of the village until Morgan rode by. It was his last ride poor fellow. Smith fired and he fell dead from the saddle.

There is but one occasion known when he met with his master before whom he quailed. This was Col. Dodge, now in command of the Dragoon Regiment. Dodge looked upon him as he really was, and treated him with contempt upon some occasion — when Smith swore, as he had often done previously with regard to others, and with fatal truth in those cases, that he would kill Dodge "on sight" — that is, the first time he met with him. The threat became generally known, and reached the ears of the person whom it most concerned. The rencontre took place at the shop of a Mr. Deaver in St. Louis from whom the story comes directly. Smith was standing in the entrance with his back to the street as Dodge rode by and he saw him. Attracted by the sound of horses feet, Smith turned round, and caught the eye of his intended victim, as the latter sprung from the saddle and presented a pistol to his breast, as his hand was already in his bosom to draw his own weapon for the fulfilment of this threat. "Move that hand one inch, in any direction" said Dodge "and I blow your brains out, you old murderer thief and swindler. The gallow is deprived of its due by your being alive, and one single movement of resistence makes you a dead man." Much language of this sort was bestowed upon him, until he said "Col. Dodge you are the only man that ever put restraint on me. You may go your ways Sir, without apprehension from me." Dodge saw that he was sincere, and putting up his weapon mounted his horse and road off. When he was out of hearing Smith turned to Deaver who had stood a trembling witness of the scene and remarked "That Col. Dodge is the most singular man I ever met with" "You had better leave him alone" replied the other. "Dont doubt it" said Smith musingly. "I am not going to interfere with him. I shall not even speak of him. He is above my mark."

Recently Smith was going up the Mississippi and when below Memphis got into a quarrel at cards and took possession of the Cabin driving the other passengers out, and standing himself in the middle of it with his pistols in his hands threatening to shoot the first man that entered. The passengers very much alarmed and knowing the character of the individual proposed to go on shore at Memphis and leave the boat altogether. "Never mind" said Captain Jackson "I will put him ashore first." Then stationing his stewards, two stout negroes at the door of the ladies cabin he called a parley with Smith and approached him in the gentlest and most conciliatory manner. To all his kind words the latter answered by oaths and vociferations, and worked himself up to such a rage that he did not perceive the approach of the negroes who springing on him unawares from behind, pinioned his arms. He was then deprived of all his weapons and put into the yawl which soon put him on terra firma to the great joy of all on board. He now says there is but one man in the world that he wants to kill and that is Jackson. This will no doubt reach the ears of the Captain, and all who know him say, that if it does he will at once undertake to anticipate the murderer and shoot him before he has an opportunity of putting his threat into execution. Should he succeed in doing so, the world will be rid of a wretch that disgraces it, by an act of as justifiable homicide as ever was committed.

Smith is upwards of seventy somewhat it is supposed & his head is snowy white. He boasts of his murders — says that he regrets but one — young Brown's who was too brave almost to be killed — that the remembrance of them has never cost him one moments sleep — and that he was justified in them all. He says he has been shot at countless times has been struck by lightning once, has had the cholera twice and the yellow fever often, and having escaped thus far anticipates living until he is an hundred years old. In his person he is slight — his face is strongly marked, and his eye remarkably brilliant. In his address he is when he pleases quiet soft spoken and gentlemanly. His very name inspires fear however, and there are but few who would not be gratified to hear of his death. He is married and has children.

It may well be asked now where are the laws — why does he still live in a civilized community? Why has he not long since suffered the assassins punishment. He has been indicted five times but has always contrived to escape. Witnesses jurymen counsel & even the bench in a newly settled country cannot be exempt from apprehensions from the violence of such a man. His very crimes make him friends of a certain description & by dint of his money & his reputation he has hitherto escaped his proper fate. It is singular that he owns a *shot* tower below St. Louis — the very employment for such a fellow.

Saturday. Nov 29th.

One of our passengers last evening told me that about a month since he was at St. Louis, and went to pass an hour on board the "Museum Boat" — a floating collection of curiosities. Here, who should he find but Black Hawk the Prophet[85] and some young Sacs, forming a part of the show and hired to be in attendance. Towards the close of the evening, Black Hawk addressed the company through an interpreter, informing them, that he was now very poor and without any money, and that if they would make up a collection for him one of his young men should dance the war dance for them. This was agreed to, the dance was danced and a collection of from $10 to $15 made on the spot. How pitiable — how melancholy — the red warrior who but a few brief months ago was at the head of a brave band of his countrymen & friends, endeavouring to wage war against the white man, their invader and their curse, is now turning his warriors into buffoons to win a scanty and miserable pittance from the victors. The Indian's fate is a melancholy one — but what help is there for it. Civilization will pass on among them and they must be trampled beneath its footsteps or flee where they cannot follow them. We have been moving, owing to our heavy load, but slowly, and it was only at one oclock today that we reached New Orleans. I had at this trip a full view of the coast as the bank of the river for a hundred miles above the city is called, and saw the steam engine at work every mile or two grinding the sugar cane. Every field was of a light green when I passed up two weeks ago, now the frost has put a stop to further growth and they are of a faded and sickly yellow.

85. Sac war chief, defeated by United States troops in 1832.

Southern Travels

Meeting my friend J B Harrison in the street as soon as I arrived I agreed to dine with him and some of his friends. We remained at the table until it was time to go to the American Theatre,[86] where I saw Mrs. Drake[87] tear a tragedy into tatters to the infinite delight of a house crowded with canaille. The Interior of the theatre is only tolerable the scenery better than we are accustomed to at the North — the french being the painters generally. The stage in the city is patronized to a considerable extent by the corporate authorities, for they have passed ordinances relating to the etiquette to be preserved, prohibiting any one sitting during the performance with his hat on — speaking loudly, thumping violently, or in any other manner disturbing or interfering with his neighbours. A copy of this ordinance is printed on the small bills so that no one can plead the excuse of ignorance. After the tragedy Harrison and myself started off to a Ball Parée[88] et Masquée in the Salle Washington[89] Rue St. Phillippe — in other words a Quadroon Ball.

86. First American theater, located on Camp Street between Gravier and Poydras, begun in May 1822 by James H. Caldwell, a local entrepreneur; it was the first building in New Orleans to be illuminated by gas. Tyrone Power performed in the American Theatre in January 1835 and described it in his *Impressions of America* (2 vols., Philadelphia, 1836, II:110) as "a large well proportioned house, with three rows of boxes, a pit, or *parquette*, as it is termed, subdivided as in the French theatre."

87. Mrs. Alexander Drake, a well-known tragedienne. In her 1834 appearance at the American Theatre, she starred in *Evadne* and in *Adelgitha*. On December 3, the drama critic of the *Bee*, Colley Cibber, wrote, "On Saturday evening Evadne was performed, in which Mrs. Drake played the principal character, and played it well, her conception of the part and reading were excellent, we were delighted with her."

88. *Trans.*: full dress ball.

89. Advertised in the *Bee* (November 29, 1834). The ballroom was designed by Latour and built in 1808-1810 on St. Philip Street between Royal and Bourbon streets as the St. Philip Street Theatre. Alterations and additions were made in 1833 by Correjolles and Chaigneau, builders. A drawing of the building appears as one of the marginal sketches on the map of New Orleans published in 1817 by J. Tanesse, city surveyor.

On entering the room, which the payment of a dollar a piece authorized us to do I was struck with its beauty and brilliancy. It is a very large one, of an oblong shape. The sides are fitted with alcoves alternating with mirrors, and are richly painted and gilded. The outline I have attempted in the marginal sketch. The ornaments are of blue and gold — and from the ceiling which is well decorated there hang five immense chandeliers blazing with cut glass and gas light — and making the brilliancy of noon day in the ball room. An orchestra of excellent music occupied an elevated gallery in the middle of one of the sides — an ante chamber contained two bars — and at the further extremity of the ball room was a large apartment opening into it under three arches corresponding to the alcoves, and similar to the opposite arches leading into the ante chamber. Windows down to the floor led out upon an iron balcony and looked out over the Southern part of the City. There many a tete à tete went forward, and doubtless many an intrigue was carried on. The beauty of this ball room far exceeds anything of the sort that we have at the North which I have seen. It was erected for the quadroons — the light mulattos of this country — who prohibited by custom and law from many of the enjoyments of the whites pass their life in a prostitution which is only the more odious, because the decencies with which it is surrounded by long usage renders it less repugnant to the moral sense and feeling than the wretched and miserable practices of the Northern cities.

There were about forty women present of all shades, from the very dark mulatto to the light quadroon whose person bore no mark of her descent, and whose degradation was a matter of tradition only. Nearly all had masks — white masks. Those who had not were young girls as yet destitute of a keeper, and who it seemed to me shewed their faces as a merchant shews samples of his wares to entice purchasers. Some of the women but not many had fine forms, and a few were graceful and elegant dancers. I was informed that this ball, by no means exhibited the handsomest, and *genteelest* of the quadroons. In the first place it was the opening Ball to which it was not fashionable for them to come — and again it was more promiscuous than those balls which they have and where a ticket is not a matter of purchase but of favor. These last are called the Society Balls — and *the best quadroon society* is to be found at them. There were no white women present; and none of the quadroons wore costume. No other disguise to the person than a domino,[90] and to the face than a mask was used.

The men were generally of very respectable appearance, all white; for *quadroon men* are *negroes* — and must be negroes in all respects. Their sisters are the favored of the family. Some of the men who took an active part in the proceedings of the evening dancing in every cotillon and talking to the girls in the intervals of the music, were past the prime of life — and looked to be fathers and grandfathers — but the most part were young men, the majority of whom seemed to be French & Spaniards. Of course there were many more lookers on, but enough took part to keep the space appropriated to dancing fully occupied. There was a waltz between every two sets — and it was really a pretty sight to see some twenty or thirty couples whirling one after another round the apartment. The waltz is different here from what it is with us. The female turns round but slowly and advances but little at each step, so that a quadroon is four times as long getting round the room as a Northern belle would be. The dance to me is a detestable one. I cannot bear it, and care not for the charge of want of civilization in declaring that nothing would ever induce me to let a wife or daughter or sister of mine join in its mazes. It is pretty, in the same way than an indecent picture may be a *pretty* one to every sense but the moral one.

Many men were masqued and in costume. Among the most conspicuous was a fellow in flesh coloured clothes fitting tight to the skin, and with ornaments of a Peruvian Indian as we sometimes see them in pictures. There were several Turks, many old men, and a capital countryman. The Peruvian got into a rare fight in the antechamber with a man who attempted to look under his mask, and when he took it off to repair damages, exhibited a bull necked savage looking person who was recognized as the keeper & bully of a tavern on the Levee. But this fellow was alone — the others in the room dressed and behaved like gentlemen. The handsomest person male or female at the Ball was a Spanish gentleman who was dressed as a woman, and was not discovered, although he wore no mask, until many of his own sex had been introduced to him, some of his acquaintances among the number, and proceeded to make love to him as a female. I had observed that the Lady had the habit of spitting on the floor and putting her foot on it and remarked upon it to a friend but it was some time after before the imposture was discovered.

90. Long, hooded cape worn as a costume.

78

Curiosity kept me looking on for sometime, and about midnight I had the chance of seeing two excellent quarrels and fights between two Frenchmen in one instance, which ended in one being knocked down, and a demand and promise of satisfaction — and in the other instance between a Spaniard & a Frenchman which ended in the arrangements for a duel. The Spaniard was so violent that he got into half a dozen quarrels and knocked down several who attempted to interfere, and who got up only to demand and be promised the reparation of their honour in mortal combat. It was curious to hear the Spaniard who cursed swore and explained in three different languages — English Spanish and French, and spoke all well. The women ran into the alcoves when the quarrels began — the nearer [scared?] the gentlemen crowded around, jumping up on the chairs and benches, and then after some five minutes of excitement, the fiddlers struck up, — the women came back to their places in the Cotillons, and everything went on as before. The quarrellers by this time having been pushed & elbowed either into the apartment at the extremity of the ball room, or the ante chamber. Below the Ball room was the supper room, where every delicacy could be procured at ten pieces for the ladies & gentlemen who are inclined to get indigestion and headaches.

Towards the end of the ball the room became very warm and the smell of the heated quadroons and mulattoes most disagreeable to one not accustomed to it. I could not bear it and went away.

As I walked down Rue Royale on my road home, I saw lights and heard the sound of music to my right in the street that runs west from the principale[91] and passing down it in front of the Theatre Orleans, I found another Quadroon Ballroom[92] as I reached the door half a dozen persons were coming out, who asked me if I had a ticket for the other place and whether I would exchange with them. This I did with a gentleman of my acquaintance and went upstairs. The scene was pretty much the same, except that here there were white women of the lowest order, — and nearly all of the women were in some sort of costume. The room was infinitely inferior to the other, and badly lighted and badly scented. It offered no inducements to remain and I returned to Bishops pretty well fatigued about one oclock.

I have seen more than I ever saw before, and my curiosity is

91. The Cabildo.

92. Orleans Ballroom on Orleans Street, designed and built by Latrobe's half-brother Henry in 1816. (See n. 51.) The ball Latrobe attended was advertised in the *Bee* (November 19, 1834).

quite gratified I assure you. One quadroon ball is enough for me. I could not get it out of my mind that those women that I saw were negroes nothing more or less; and I could only feel contempt for those whom I saw paying them the attention and respect which should belong to female virtue alone. I pity the poor creatures whom the white man's sins makes infamous, and devotes to prostitution from their cradle. I could not for worlds have the feelings which would be mine, were my eye as it fell upon my child, to see the future mistress of the white man — living with him in an intercourse, sanctioned by no one ceremony — unholy and accursed. My feeling for the quadroon woman is a feeling of compassion — for her keeper one of a very different character. The sin is his, far more than hers.

One thing is very certain, — New Orleans would have far less of the picturesque if it had more of morals to recommend it. This much however I can safely say of it, that I never was in a more quiet, or better ordered city at those periods when riot is rifest ordinarily, and when the night is made the period of noise and disturbance. Except a few drinking houses, principally on Levée Street, and the gaming houses — you walk through the streets after ten oclock without meeting an individual or hearing a sound. Everything is still — and I would quite as soon trust myself in any part of New Orleans after that hour, as I would in any of the Northern cities. So far too as my personal comfort is concerned I have been most hospitably and kindly treated, — and shall not soon forget the attentions that I have received.

November 30th. Sunday.

This morning I went to the Catholic Cathedral, and heard a sermon in French. It is [a] most miserable looking affair inside, having no pretention to architectural beauty and without any of the rich ornament that makes the other Catholic churches that I have seen in Canada and the United States imposing and attractive. It is very dirty looking, and the walls which were originally painted have been defaced, and wear a shabby look. There are three altars; one at the end of the grand Aisle, and the others on each side Aisle. The pews were tolerably well filled, and I recognized in some of them the quadroons that I had seen without masks on the preceding evening. The aisles were filled, mostly with mulatto and negro women sitting on chairs and dressed in the most party coloured garments — looking as gay as a bed of tulips in full bloom.

When the service was over and the congregation rose, it was amusing to look into the aisles and see the shouldering of chairs that took place, — for the crowd being too great to permit the chair or stool to be carried out by the side of the person it was lifted, legs uppermost overhead, presenting the appearance of a chevaux de frise.[93] A good many elderly coloured women with long veils on, and some young and well dressed quadroon girls had little negroes with them in the aisles who shouldered their chairs for them, but the greater number carried for themselves.

At the foot of the aisles were two men in uniforms with espontoons[94] whose office was to keep silence and preserve decorum. When the bell rung before the elevation of the host they brought their weapon to a carry, and when the bell rung for the elevation they dropped a handkerchief on the pavement, knelt on it on one knee, and lowered the spear point to the ground.

The preacher was a man of abilities and his sermon was an impressive one. He sat down very often during its delivery and bobbed up again, in a most ungraceful and undignified manner, — for he spoke without interruption when seated. The sermon was not a long one, and the whole ceremony was over before 11 o'clock.

I saw the finest looking woman in this church that I have yet seen in the southern country. She was in black, without a bonnet but with a long black veil that hung down from behind the comb in her hair. She was above the common size — had beautiful feet and ankles, which her dress was calculated to exhibit, — and stood with great grace and dignity during the whole service. She seemed a native, and a Spaniard. Her face was not strictly handsome, — but there was about her person and carriage a commanding yet feminine dignity that I have rarely if ever seen before. I enquired who she was but could not learn. She was probably in the middle class from her dress & the fact that she had no pew, but performed her devotions in the aisle.

After church I walked along Rue de Chartres to the New Orleans & Pontchartrain railroad depot[95] and buying a ticket for 37½ cents, or in the phrase of the country three bits, found my self in ten minutes four miles off at Lake Pontchartrain. There is a large hotel here with several other buildings, put up as places of

93. *Trans.*: protective line of spikes on top of a wall.
94. Half pike carried by a subordinate officer.
95. Located on Elysian Fields Avenue. The tracks ran along the avenue to Milneburg on the shore of Lake Pontchartrain. The company was chartered in 1830, and the road opened for business on April 23, 1831.

amusement[96] — together with the shops and carriage houses of the railroad Company. A very long pier upon piles extends to water of a sufficient depth for the steamboats and schooners that navigate the lake, for whose accommodations breakwaters also of piles have been built at the end and sides of the pier as per margin. Upon

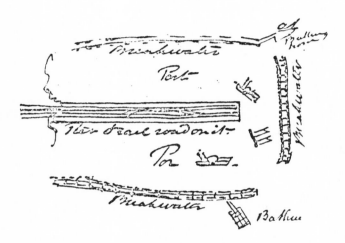

getting out of the car which stopped at the ticket office at the beginning of the pier, I looked at my watch & found that agreably to the advertisement of the hours of passing to & from between New Orleans & the lake I had some time to spare so I walked to the end of the pier which was rendered quite lively by the presence of three or four steam boats and some half dozen sloops and schooners. Here and there the broad and now tranquil waters of the lake were dotted with sails, the sky forming the greater part of the horizon, which was completed by long and dark lines of low woods which rose from swamps and stretched for some distance to the right and left of me. On turning about to regain the cars, I saw them flying off some half mile or more ahead of me on their way back to the city. I had no remedy but patience — and soothing myself with the reflection that the same hurry which carried them away half an hour before their time would soon bring them back again, I walked to the tavern and took my seat in the porch. Here I was disturbed by a constant firing which seemed close at my ear,

96. The Washington Hotel was located on the lakefront across from the Milneburg depot. Harriet Martineau, in her *Retrospect of Western Travel* (2 vols., London, 1838, II:123), described the hotel "with its galleries and green blinds, built for coolness, where gentlemen from New Orleans go to eat fish and bathe."

and having borne it for some time I got up to see where it came from. Turning the corner near which I was seated, I saw painted over a low browed door "Pistoll Shuting" in what the French man who made the sign thought was English, and underneath "Tir au pistolet" I went in and soon saw the cause of my annoyance. There were two targets placed ten paces from a small [counter?] on which was a plate of pistol bullets, and over it a powder horn — and from the two a man was loading one after another four duelling pistols, which he handed to two persons practicing at the targets on either side of the loader. One of these was a plain cast iron plate blackened with a vertical white line drawn through the middle of it and in the centre a round mark rather larger than a dollar. This last was movable and so arranged with spring behind the target that when struck it caused a catch to fly back and a piece of painted tin called "le pavillon" to start up above the target. The targets themselves were of cast iron. The second was different from that just described in having the outline of a man standing sideways with a pistol held with a straight arm pointing to the ground — and the bulls eye, which being struck started the pavillon was on the heart. The politeness of the Frenchman who offered me the pistols induced me to take a few shots, and having hit the centre once I paid my four bits, for eight times, I think, and gave up my place to new comers. I need hardly tell you that I fired at the plain target, having no desire to practice even upon the outlines of one of my fellow beings. Leaving the "Tir" I got a piece of paper from the bar and set about a sketch of the pier. While thus engaged it became darker and darker every moment, and the atmosphere appeared a peculiar and sickly hue, and yet still the sun cast shadows on the ground, though by the time I had finished my sketch they were ragged and confused along their edges. I was quite ignorant of any immediate cause for all this until I heard the bar keeper call out for a piece of burnt glass and then at once knew there must be an eclipse of the sun. And in the truth it was, "The great Eclipse," as the newspapers called it, of which I was a spectator. Keeping but little count of events, and seeing no newspapers in my recent travels, where it was mentioned, I had not been aware of its approach. It is not my purpose to go into a detail of it, how many digits were eclipsed, how long it lasted, &c. The Almanacks for that. The marginal figure represents what appeared to me to be the proportion of the part obscured — and not far from the little remnant of sun that the impolite moon like a person

walking between one & the fire, left to warm us mortals below, I saw the evening star most distinctly. But apart from the science of the subject there was a powerful effect produced on the mind by the ghastly sickly and decaying hue that was spread over the landscape. The bare and melancholy shores of the lake to which the dim atmosphere gave a more gloomy appearance even than they ordinarily possessed, — the breathless calm upon the waters, the utter silence that prevailed — the want of human beings to animate the scene — all made me feel as though I stood where the plague had swept away its myriads and desolation reigned supreme. Pestilence too found its ordinary home in the unhealthy swamps and their stagnant waters — on every side — and the great City — not far distant was the strangers lazar house. These facts added force to what imagination created in my mind, and I walked to the margin of the waters and looked out upon them, and strained my eyes as though I might see the spirit of destruction sweeping across the tranquil surface of the lake. But it came not; the air lightened again — a light breeze darkened the waters, and the engine and its train of cars arriving from New Orleans, filled the pier with a crowd of gay and laughing people, who effectually extinguished the sparks of poetry which had been twinkling within me, and satisfied me that good company and a prospect of arriving on time for a good dinner to which I had been invited in the City were far preferable to the magnificence of desolation. Ten minutes afterwards I was walking quietly along the Rue Royale in New Orleans. It was Sunday & I saw a crowd at a "Flying horse" house, or shed, on a vacant lot where sailors were whirling round, swearing and drinking and idlers of all colours gazing in envy or admiration. Half a square off; I saw the congregation coming out of the Ursuline chapel.[97]

After dinner I went to the Opera to see Le Pre aux Clercs. The

97. Located on Ursulines Street between Chartres and Decatur (Levee), adjacent to the old Ursuline Convent. Illustrated in *The Historical Epitome of the State of Louisiana* (New Orleans, 1840, 309), it was described as "exceedingly plain and unpretending in its exterior, and chiefly interesting from its associations." Some of the old chapel walls stood until October 1985 when demolished by the archdiocese.

house was crowded to overflowing and the ladies were numerous & brilliantly dressed. I had to stand during the performance, and left the Theatre with my back almost broken. After a supper at Guillaume's I went to bed in good time.

December 1st Monday.

Today I lounged about the town until dinner time when I went down the coast to the house of Mr. Jno. George[98] where I dined. He has an immense sugar Refinery, upon the principle of using steam, which I went through & which is in itself well worth a ride from town to visit. On my way I passed the house of the woman Lalaurie, which was torn to pieces by the people on the discovery of the cruel treatment that she bestowed on her slaves.[99] I learned from the gentleman who accompanied me that her name before her marriage to Lalaurie had been Blanc, and I recognized in it the name of a female neighbour of my fathers when he resided in New Orleans who personally superintended the beating of her negroes in a yard exposed to the view of all who lived around her. Upon inquiring I found that the woman Lalaurie "Lucrece Borgia" as she is most generally called now was the same Madame Blanc of whom I had so often heard my mother speak as a fiend incarnate.[100]

A negro man some short time since struck a white one with a stick of wood in a moment of excitement without doing him any injury. He was *tried* by three jurors before the parish judge forthwith, and hung *toute suite* — according the law in such case made and provide by the [*wise and humane?*] policy of the state.*
Had the woman Lalaurie been tried for crimes towards her unfortunate negroes of a far deeper dye than murder, a pecuniary fine which with her great fortune she would have laughed at would have been her only punishment. And yet the woman Lalaurie and the negro who was executed for raising his hand against a white

*I tell you this as it was told me by [L. C.?] Harrison of the firm of Harrison, Brown & Company of N.O.

98. John George, a director of the New Orleans Sugar Refinery.

99. On April 10, 1834, the Lalaurie house at the corner of Royal and Gov. Nicholls streets caught fire. Neighbors rushing in to extinguish the blaze found slaves in chains and apparently suffering from ill-treatment. As a result of newspaper accounts of the incident, a mob broke in and sacked the house. In 1837 the ruined house was sold by Madame Lalaurie to Pierre E. Trastour, an architect-builder who restored it, adding the elaborate interior plasterwork as well as a rear addition and the third floor.

100. Before her marriage to Dr. Louis Lalaurie in 1825, Madame Lalaurie, née Delphine Macarty, was married first to Ramón de López y Angula who died in 1804, and then to Jean Blanque who died in 1816.

man, will stand as equals before Him who made them both. The Lex humana & the Lex Divina are widely different in Louisiana.

December 2nd Tuesday.

I have staid at Bishop's Hotel on this visit to New Orleans in preference to going to a private Boarding house. It is an immense building and is always crowded during the winter months. There is much confusion and no comfort at all — not through any fault of the keeper, but from the necessity of the case — for I hold it to be a rule that after a Tavern gets beyond a certain size it gets as a matter of course to be uncomfortable. The most striking part of this establishment is the Bar — a large and well finished room of perhaps 80 x 40. and which is thronged from 10 oclock in the morning until the same hour at night with people from all parts of the Country talking till they are dry, and then drinking to talk again, or which is not infrequent drinking without the excuse of "Spitting for penny bits,"[101] before they begin. The ordinary number of glasses of drink sold in the day is 1200 — at 12½ cents each. There had been as many as 2000, and very frequently 1750. This I learned from Bishop himself.

At ½ past one oclock I left the depot of the Rail Road on my way to Mobile, and embarked at the Lake on board the steam boat Watchman which carries the mail between the two places. I was quite unwell with all the symptoms of a very heavy cold or influenza creeping over me fast. But I determined not to be sick if I could help it in New Orleans where association of ideas alone would have gone far to kill me. The Watchman did not get off until late in the afternoon — and I got into my berth with a raging headache and high fever as soon as we left the pier. The engine was a low pressure one, and sadly out of order; the boiler leaked and every now and then the works would come to a stop of themselves. The jar too was very great, and every one on board became nervously excited, and fearful of accident. Just as I was getting into a doze about 10 oclock two of the passengers seated themselves opposite the head of my berth and began to talk of yellow fever. One of them had had it in the summer, and proceeded to detail all his symptoms with the most provoking precision — and over and over again. He had first felt an approaching cold — he said. This made me prick my ears. Then

101. Colloquial expression meaning dry-mouthed, that is, in need of a drink.

after a day or two a tremendous headache — worse and worse
thinks I — then a violent fever — and I began to count my pulse.
Then pains in the back — my own was aching most sorely. Then
in the limbs — fortunately I had not got to that — and then
delirium — and I began to try if I could think clearly, and thought
& thought again until I almost doubted my own collectedness. I
wished the talkers to the devil, and became satisfied that I had all
the symptoms of yellow fever, and tried to make up my mind as to
what I should do now that my head was still clear enough for
thought. I was in the middle of the lake in the mail boat — so that
I had no chance of turning back. I was to be landed on the shore
where there were no accommodations to take stage there for
Mobile, and to travel thirty miles through a wilderness. I became
puzzled — but felt calm enough notwithstanding to understand fully
my situation, and to get up and take three Lees pills — the only
medicine I had with me. I had just crept into my berth again, when
a shriek of pain from the deck brought most of the passengers into
the middle of the cabin floor, for it would have aroused the seven
sleepers themselves had they heard it. It proceeded from one of the
negro firemen who had refused to do his duty and had been struck
by the mate violently, and as it was said, so as to draw blood. One
of the passengers a young man with tallow coloured hair, who had
been up and down some dozen times with the dysentery, and was as
nervous as he could be, woke the Captain who went on deck and
in a few minutes all was quiet again. We had not got composed
however, before there was another tumult above among the hands
and we heard the appalling cry of "a man overboard" followed by
the trampling of many feet, the lowering of a boat and the loud
commands called for by the occasion. It appeared that the negro
who had been struck had again refused to perform his duty and
when the mate attempted again to strike him had held his hand
and stood on the Defensive, which only made the officer more
enraged, and the negro escaping from him, ran to the side and
leaped over the railing into the lake. When we got upon the deck
the engine had stopped and backed water, and the yawl was pulled
by the oarsmen round the spot where the fireman was last seen to
rise. It was a sad and gloomy night. The steam boat was as silent as
the grave, everyone holding his breath to hear whether a shout or
cry from the negro would be a guide to those who were out to save
him. But few stars were visible — and the black volumes of smoke
from the chimney of the boat, produced by the pitchpine used in

firing took a direction which was over the spot where the yawl was making its search, and fell heavily down towards the waters, as though they would have formed a funeral pall for the poor wretch who had thus made himself a free man. But the rolling of the oars was the only sound heard, except when the steersman of the boat would hussa loudly to direct the attention of the negro. It all was in vain. The fireman rose but once to the surface immediately after he first sunk, & before assistance could be rendered — uttered but one faint cry — and after searching for near half an hour — the yawl was hauled up — the engine set in motion, and the Watchman moved forward on her course. You may imagine, my dear fellow, that this sad event coming on top of the yellow fever conversation was not calculated to quiet me — and I wish no one to pass a more wretched night than I did. I did pass through it however and saw the sun rise just as it was announced that we were in sight of the landing place to which we were bound.

Wednesday December 3rd

Soon after sunrise we moored to the end of a long narrow pier of piles that projected from the low flat shore to a depth of water sufficient for steam boat navigation, and paying four bits to the steward to take care of my baggage and bring it after me I hurried at the risk of falling into the marsh half a dozen times, over the loose boards of the ricketty pier to secure a comfortable seat in the stage, which you may be satisfied, I greeted the sight of with great joy. I found it on the shore ready to receive the passengers, and got into it with some doubt whether I should be able to bear the ride in it to Mobile. There was no crowd assembled to see its departure. A low house with the accompanying outbuildings all looking deserted were the only evidences of civilization which the country afforded, except the steam boat the stage the pier & the passengers. A dark green belt of pine woods stretched far to the right and left in the deep recesses of which the lightly marked and seldom traveled road was soon lost to sight.

Our stage was a new and very excellent one — but our team as sorry a collection of beasts, altho one was named Eclipse[102] and another Bucephalus[103] as I ever saw hitched to the mail. Ten of us however with much baggage were safety drawn by it through an unbroken forest of pines for thirteen miles over a level road to the

---

102. Eighteenth-century English racehorse who won all his races.
103. Alexander the Great's war horse.

relay house on the banks of Dog river creek. Here we found a stage driver and hostler only, but got a cup of decent coffee, and a better set of horses, which carried us at a clever rate to Mobile. Ten miles from Mobile we passed through Spring Hill, an elevated tract of country possessing fine water and the resort of the citizens in the unhealthy summers. From Spring Hill to Mobile, the road on either side is lined with cottages and country seats some of them extremely beautiful and presenting the appearance of a continuous village. The road itself is without any exception the best I ever traveled over, being made of the shells which are found in great numbers on the salt water, and which after being for sometime put down form a surface as smooth as a board and very hard. The motion of the heavily loaded stage was not as rough on this road as the motion of a rail road car on the best constructed rails.

We stopped in Mobile at the Mansion house, where I determined to remain for some days to get rid of the influenza with which I had been attacked in New Orleans, for by this time my yellow fever fright was pretty well over. I could not have made choice of a better stopping place. There is but one hotel in the United States that can be compared to the Mansion house, and that is the Tremont at Boston. The charges, true, are exorbitant; but one must pay for comfort highly every where in the South. I am not going to give you the statistics of Mobile. You can learn these from books &c. It is a bustling thriving town supported by a back country of cotton growers, and being the depot of all that is produced on the waters of the Alabama Tombigbee, Black Warrior & Coosa rivers & their tributaries. Although so near to New Orleans it is not such a city as that is, in the manners of the people. The American population has the ascendancy in numbers & influence — and the habits and customs are like those of any other American city of the same size. I found the wharves covered with cotton & sea vessels and steam boats constantly arriving and departing.

In page 21 [p. 24] of these memoranda, I have found great fault with the English for not putting a light on the Island of Abaco, or suffering the U.S. to do it. Since I have been in Mobile, however, I have seen the advertisement of "His Majesty's Government" for proposals to erect two on the Islands in that quarter — and withdraw as in honor bound my querulous complainings on page aforesaid 21.

Today, while in a book store, a cotton factor came in with a memorandum in his hand which he peered at most attentively through his spectacles, and then asked, after mumbles — Hams — flour — cotton bagging — Ah yes here, here it is — Have you got the Star Spangled Banner — The Soldier Tired — and Liberty's Home?" "No Sir said the Mobilian Bookseller. Those things are published in the Western Songster, and of course are *damned low*, and do not appear as promiscuous music on the shelves of a genteel store"!! So you see, what the Star Spangled Banners come to — out here.

Dec 6th Saturday

I had taken my passage in the Steam Boat Dover intending to go up the Alabama river to Montgomery and save the disagreables of a land journey of two hundred miles — but upon going on board this evening, I found there was every probability of great detention on the river, so I determined to push on by the mail & start tomorrow by that conveyance. I am pretty sure of being in time for the Charleston & Norfolk packet which I would not be if I was to go up the Alabama and get aground on the voyage — for an indefinite period.

Sunday 7th December.

This morning at the suggestion of Mr. Baker the British consul at Mobile I provided myself with a pocket flask of good brandy with which to dilute the wretched water that he told me I would find on the road & a stone jug of good sherry wine. I added of my own accord a pound of bologna sausage and a quantity of crackers. Mrs. Gilliat with great kindness insisted upon contributing to my preparations a "comfort" of cotton wadded between calico and as large as a single matrass so that I found myself provided with every thing that could be anticipated as necessary to my well being on my proposed journey.

The day turned out to be dark & uncomfortable, a strong wind from the South East bringing with it occasional clouds of mist that at times wholly obscured the horizon and penetrated the clothing quite as much as a heavy rain. At half past four I went on board the Steam boat Emmeline, which was to convey the mail to Stockton on the Tensaw River about forty miles from Mobile. The boat was the smallest I had yet been in, miserably dirty having a cramped cabin with eight or ten berths, the bedding of which looked as if it had been used by the firemen for weeks. Our rate of motion too, did not exceed six miles at furthest. Bad as the berths were I selected one of them with a determination to sleep if I could for the last time in a bed before the day and night travel of the coming journey.

We passed slowly out of the narrow and melancholy entrance of Mobile river, whose channel was defined by the black and bare trunks of trees which the floods of many springs and falls had deposited on the shallow places of the stream. Turning then to the Eastward we passed the mouth of Spanish river, forming with the Alabama the muddy island before Mobile, and changing our course to the North entered the Tensaw River, and followed its windings to Stockton, a small settlement of recent origin on its left Bank and where our land journey was to commence. On our way we stopped to land passengers at Blakely a petty and [demeaning?] village, pregnant with Cholera & yellow fever.

We reached Stockton at ten oclock. A huge fire had been built on the edge of the river to direct us to the landing, and in a short time our baggage was fastened to the stage which waited for us, sheltered from a heavy rain by a large tree, — the whip was cracked, a long stick of lightwood, served for a flambeau, and off we started across the *"railroads"* in the vicinity at the rate of 2½ miles an hour. My companions were three in number. One of them was a young storekeeper, on his way to Claiborne in Alabama, who had the cholic, & looked very dismally, and who had the first *"shot"* from my *"pocket pistol."* The other two were negro dealers or traders returning from a profitable trip to the West. They had disposed of their merchandise earlier than usual and were hurrying home to Virginia to pass Christmas among their friends. The eldest of them was as deaf as a post — an inveterate smoker, of an irritable temper, and a perfect walking collection of all the nasty vulgar & obscene wit and poetry of the day, which he did not hesitate to repeat at all times without much regard to company, and as he could not always distinguish whether those around him were talking or not, or what they were talking about he sometimes broke in with his story or song in the most malapropos place, and interrupted some sufficiently grave and proper discourse with bawdy ribaldry. He was a singularly sober man, and never swore, spoke reverently enough too, of sacred things, but his beastiality of language was unsurpassable. He might have been accounted good looking but for the sad preponderance of the animal in his physiognomy. His companion who was also his cousin was quiet & well behaved, and but slightly tinctured with the others proclivities.

Southern Travels

They had started from home in good clothes but were now shabby enough. Coming from New Orleans, directly, they had a preference to me in the choice of seats, which they availed themselves of by ensconcing themselves in the back one while I and the cholicky clerk took possession opposite. The stage was well enough and better than I had expected to find, although the sash of one door window being lost its place was supplied by a piece of Canvass, into which some previous passenger, in a hurry to look out, had made a long gash with his knife. The other door window had its sash but was deficient in the glass which had long been broken through.

The pine stick that was carried along side of the driver gave a brilliant light, better than any lamp that we could have obtained — but we were still better lighted, when on meeting the Southern stage a short distance from Stockton, we got from the driver, a grating, cup shaped and about six inches broad at the top, fastened to a long rod which being placed under the driver's cushion kept the pot or grating at such distance as he desired from the side of the stage. The grating was filled with light wood and gave a most brilliant illumination to our road extending far on either side into the recesses of the forest. The motion of the stage fed the flame with a constant draft, and the fuel was from time to time supplied from a bag under the drivers feet. On one occasion we all jumped from the stage to avoid an upset and I walked a short distance ahead. It was a novel sight to see the carriage dashing along the road with its strange lamp gear leaving a long train of smoke behind it spangled with the sparks from the pine and giving to the boles of the trees as they received and then lost the red glare of the light — the appearance of tall spectres dancing in the gloom. Here and there too, an owl disturbed by the infrequent visit of the brightness of day at the depth of midnight would screech forth his astonishment in his half human tones, and sweep with a dull flapping of his wings still deeper among the pines.

We rattled along very fast changing horses every ten and twelve miles, until daylight — soon after which we stopped at the breakfasting house, a sorry cabin in a scanty clearing to the left of our road. Here we all laughed at each others appearance as we emerged from our dark and confined stage; for the pine smoke had converted us into negroes, so far as colour went. We washed ourselves as clean as we could, and promised, the next time to have the fire pot carried to Leeward, and not to windward as it had been tonight. Our fare consisted of poor coffee, hominy — hog in several shapes — such as sausages, spare ribs and pickled chine, and Indian bread — I paid fifty cents for the privilege of sitting down in a violent draft from the open door to the immense fireplace. Eat I could not.

After breakfast, with a fresh and excellent team we pursued our way through the pine forest, with no other incident worth notice, than that the driver chose to run a race for many miles with a two horse phaeton to the great risk of our necks as he whirled us among the trees, — and at two oclock we reached Claiborne,[104] a small village on the Alabama river, the depot for the cotton that is raised in the neighbourhood. It was not my luck to see any of the plantations, for not a single dwelling, except the relay houses did we pass during the morning. At Claiborne we got a tolerable dinner, which we sat down to with an odd set of folks, all cotton worshippers, for they talked of nothing else, thought of nothing else and no doubt dreamt of nothing but long & short staple, and twenty cents per pound. Here our cholicky friend got out, and in his place we took *on board* as it is termed here, a Col Fox, who proposed to accompany us as far as Burnt Corn.[105] The elder trader had become familiar during the morning and finding it difficult to "call my name" dubbed me major to which I made no objection, trusting that my title might perhaps serve me in stead. Now Col. Fox was but a militia colonel, and as the deaf Trader told him that I was in the "States' service," I was treated by him with profound consideration, which became almost overpowering when he found out by his cross questioning that I had married the daughter of the gentleman after whom Claiborne was called. Col. Fox had sold his horse "in town" and was on his way home with his saddle in the stage. We set him down at a comfortable looking log house on the way side about dusk, and soon after found ourselves at a house and some outbuildings which went by the name of "Burnt Corn." I ought not to forget to mention that in the afternoon we passed through Centreville the County town of Monroe county — and a new creation in the forest. Not a house was more than a year old and the trees had only been cleared from out the public square and on the sites of the dwellings. They were some forty or fifty in number, and their appearance was striking and picturesque. At one time Claiborne was the seat of Justice of the county. Local interests

104. On the river bluff is the site of Fort Claiborne, built in 1813 by General Ferdinand Leigh Claiborne, Mrs. Latrobe's father.
105. Scene of a Creek Indian victory on July 27, 1813.

however had established it among the pine woods at Centreville, and a courthouse, two Taverns and some half dozen stores made a very respectable appearance in the wilderness.

Burnt Corn offered nothing to detain us — save the tradition of the Indian skirmish in which the savages had succeeded in setting fire to the corn cribs of the settlers, and thus furnished the incident from which the place derived its present name. After a meagre supper, I rolled myself up in my comfort, thanking my kind friend Mrs. Gilliat for it as I did so, and dozed in a fitful slumber through the night notwithstanding the thumping and bumping and jumping of the stage over corduroy roads, pine roots, — and well washed gullies — and deaf too to the clamour of the drivers at every changing place who spent from half an hour to an hour each time by the side of their blazing fire of lightwood, in gossipping & swearing and making up their minds to get forward. We had the fire pot again tonight, but took care that it was placed where its smoke could not make negroes of us. The negro traders took turns in the bottom of the stage on bundles of corn fodder leaving me a whole seat to myself. I have slept worse than I did to night. I was tired enough to have slept in a ditch.

December 9th.

I did not get wide awake until near ten oclock when the driver told us that an hour would bring us to Greenville and our breakfast. I had become wearied of the pine woods, and the prospect of a collection of houses roused me completely. In an hour we did get to Greenville, and after waiting until near twelve oclock got something to eat — hog and hominy and cornbread being still preponderant in the bill of fare. The night had been very cold, so I went to a shop in the village and bought a blanket, and two yards of flannel for leggins or wrappers. Red was the only colour I could obtain that was suitable, so that I now cut a most conspicuous figure about my lower extremities to the vast amusement of the boys and girls who see me pass along, and to the great envy of the Indians that I meet with on the way. The tavern at Greenville was originally intended for a comfortable house, but there was not now a single sash in the lower story, and as the morning was cold, my seat at the breakfast table with a window open at my back one on each side and an open door in front was not the most comfortable. And yet the people around seemed quite surprised at my keeping on my coat & cloak during the meal.

On getting again into the stage I found a lady & gentleman & a young girl occupying the back seat so that my two companions and myself had to squeeze into the front one. This was against all the rules of staging which gave the choice of seats to those who have traveled furthest on the route. But ladies being in the case we did not care to oust the gentleman, and off we rattled, with the recollection of a bad breakfast, and the discomfort of an inconvenient seat — to improve our good fellowship towards the strangers. For some time we rode sulkily along. The females were silent as they could be — but the man was a jolly soul and the party being bound for a wedding and in rare spirits an equilibrium of temper was established in a short time between the fore and hind seats of the carriage, and conversation gradually became continuous. I learned a good deal of the country through which we were traveling before we got to the house of the bride, and had the story of many a hunt and many a race related with a spirit and force which it requires the peculiar phraseology of the country to impart — or which I would attempt to imitate. Your selfish, silent traveller is but a poor acquirer of knowledge. Like the perfumer who thrusting his nose into the first pot of almond paste that he examined, fancied as he smelt all his stock of sweets that he had nothing but almond pomatum in his collection — so the traveller who looks only, and does not talk or listen carries about with him the feelings & prejudices of the only land he knows, his home, and is wholly unable to appreciate the peculiar characteristics of the new people among whom he finds himself. I am at times when travelling, of a sulky silent spirit, for I become tired and wearied in body and my body makes my spirit pay for its sufferings — but I struggle ag'st the feeling, for in proportion as I yield to it I become ennuyee and uncomfortable. But let me get on towards Montgomery.

Towards evening the wedding guests left us, and we once more had the stage to ourselves, and assumed our positions of the preceding night. We slept soundly for sometime, and were awoke by hearing the driver say that we had lost the linch pin of one of the forewheels and had been travelling for some time without one. It was nearly dark and no blacksmith nigh when this discovery was made, so that our only resource was a stout wedge of oak which we trusted to until we reached the changing house, and found a blacksmith who soon put us in safety. The country through which we have been travelling has been generally covered with a growth of gigantic pines with here and there tracts of oak and hickory land, where clearings were to be found and the cotton gin & press were in busy motion. We have not passed through the best part of Alabama by any means, and the excellence of the roads over which we have been travelling is in part to be attributed to the cold dry soil on which they are located.

At 10 oclock we were roused by the drivers horn as we drew nigh to Montgomery, and were rejoiced when, soon afterwards we thawed ourselves, for the night was cold & damp before a blazing fire in the principle inn of the place. Montgomery is near the head waters of the Alabama river, and at the limit of Steam Boat Navigation. It is the Depot of the cotton which is raised for many miles around it, and is a rapidly increasing and very thriving town. Boats sometimes ascend the river to Wetumpka some miles above, but nothing can interfere with the growth of Montgomery, which will before long be second only to Mobile in the State of Alabama.

After waiting long enough for the Post Office arrangements to be completed, we were hurried into the stage and started for Fort Mitchell a distance of ninety miles. Our company was now increased by two persons, — the one a country doctor going as far as the breakfasting stand and the other, a man with an immensely long name which I have forgotten and whose occupation I could not by any means ascertain. The Doctor was quiet when awake, but snored like an elephant when asleep & also eructated most unpleasantly during his dreams. I trod on his toes, for he sat on the seat before, and kicked his shins to wake him from time to time, but he would sleep and snore & belch kicking & treading notwithstanding.

Ten miles from Montgomery we came to [Line?] creek which in summer is a dry ditch, but at this season was filled with water so as to be crossed only in a ferry boat. It divides the Creek nation of Indians from the other part of Alabama, and upon crossing it I found myself once more, where Indian laws and customs still kept a slight foothold in the vast forests which overshadowed the land. We got out of the stage before the creek was crossed, and walked for some distance to the huge fire that was kindled before the change house on the opposite side. It was about 2 oclock in the morning. The air blew very cold down the water course and chilled us through and the stars overhead shone with a brilliancy that I thought belonged only to a northern atmosphere. We therefore crowded round the fire and roasted back & front and sides alternately like geese in the process of cooking and then sat on the ground that the soles of our feet might receive the generous heat of the [?]. Ten minutes would have been ample time to change the horses and resume the route — but the two drivers were old acquaintances, and had much to talk about, & never dreamt of stirring for two hours after we got to the fire. The drivers too, we found were lord paramounts in this country and there was no arguing with them. They were not ready to go they said; and they would not go until they were ready, and if we did not like our conveyance we might find a better. A poor consolation in a forest in Alabama, and one which certainly never would have been offered in the streets of Baltimore or Washington where such things exist as opposition lines of coaches. For my own part I left my companions lounging by the fire, burning and turning and unwilling to leave their positions, and got into the stage, when after amusing myself for sometime with the picturesque effect of the light upon the huts where the horses were kept — the trees and the rushing stream, I wrapt myself in my cloak — made a pillow of my comfort and went sound asleep — dreamed of my wife and children — had happy and fair visions and was as comfortable as a king until roused by "Helloa Major you take a dev'lish sight of room." The eldest negro trader was accosting me — and making place for him beside me the stowage of the stage was completed and away we rattled, over a long causeway that banished sleep from my eyes for the rest of the night.

Tuesday Dec' 16th.

Soon after sunrise this morning the stage stopped to breakfast at Durants, a wretched house open on all sides to the winds of Heaven, and belonging to a white man who had intermarried with a half breed Indian woman. His daughter, quite a pretty quadroon presided at a breakfast table better filled than was to have been expected from the appearance of the premises, and her cousin, even better looking served us with hot smoking cakes from the griddle in the adjoining kitchen. A ride of some five hours brought us to Fort Hull, a collection of log dwellings surrounded by the remains of a bastioned breast work, and erected during one of the campaigns of the last war.[106] We changed horses here and continued through the pine forest until four oclock in the afternoon when we reached

106. Built in 1813 on the Old Federal Road by General John Floyd during the Creek Indian War.

Hinjes, a transparent loghouse on the road side and found dinner prepared for us. I soon dispatched my portion of the meal and spying a pretty well dressed woman in the next room with a neat foot that would have passed muster anywhere and with a carriage and tournure[107] more than ordinarily good, I set to work to make an acquaintance, and had near an hours very pleasant conversation, madame being quite au fait to the usages of good company. I could not rest till I learned how such a flower became planted among the forests of the Creek nation — and I learnt the story. A handsome husband — somewhat of a *mauvais sujet*[108] — great affection — pliable temper &c, &c — and ascertained that three years residence had so habituated her to the place that she had ceased to think of the more civilized society that she had left "all for love." "I wonder at myself" she said "when I think where I am, and where & what I was before I came here — but I don't want to change. I am quite contented. To be sure these Indians are great thieves and leave one no peace of ones life. They kill the cows steal the poultry and are very devils when they can get drink — but still I have learned how to get along with them and they give me but little trouble. I'm not in a palace either," she added looking round at the glassless window near which she sat, the open seams in the floor and the smoked rafters "but still when one's content, that's enough." The lady was a philosopher — more of one than her dress seemed to indicate. I could have rather sworn she was a coquette. At all events she was the prettiest thing I had seen for three hundred miles.

I was quite sorry to leave the dining house — but the driver blew his horn, and away we rattled over a fine road through an unbroken forest towards Fort Mitchell. We were most of the time within sight of large fires made by the "movers" who were "camping out" for the night on their journey from Virginia North & South Carolina to Alabama Mississippi or Texas.[109] The groups which these emigrants formed were highly picturesque, and as it was still early in the evening when we passed them, we saw men women & children busy at work in preparing their food, or making their arrangements

107. *Trans.*: figure.
108. *Trans.*: worthless character.
109. Throughout his presidency (1828-36), Andrew Jackson followed a broad policy of extinguishing Indian land titles and removing the Indian population. During his tenure 94 Indian treaties were signed with a consequent movement of Indians to the western territories. See Robert V. Remini, *Andrew Jackson and the Course of American Freedom, 1822-1832*, (New York, 1981); and Ronald N. Satz, *American Indian Policy in the Jacksonian Era*, (Lincoln, Neb., 1975).

for rest during the night. At eight oclock we stopped to change horses and found that the king bolt of the stage had broken in two. Fortunately we had a spare one with us, and after some little delay in substituting it for the invalid one we resumed our road and reached Fort Mitchell, a small collection of indifferent buildings by 10 oclock. In a cleared space to the north or the road we saw numerous lights with figures passing frequently before them and heard the confused hum which proceeds from the voices of many people gathered together. It was an encampment of between three and four hundred Indians who were collected here by the orders of government previous to emigrating from their country to the lands prepared for them to the West of the Mississippi. I had seen many small parties during the day all directing their steps to the rendevous at Fort Mitchell. On my journey to Natchez in 1832 I had passed through the Choctaw nation, and now found myself among the Creeks. Both too, were on the eve of emigration when I saw them, so that I had opportunities of observing the people better than are ordinarily enjoyed by the traveller who is carried by the mail post haste through the Indian Territory. I have found no occasion to alter the opinion I expressed in 1832 with regard to the Indians and their relations to the government and citizens of the United States.

At Fort Mitchell we got an addition of two passengers which filled our coach. The one was a talking boasting fellow who wanted to enter into an argument with me on the subject of the Bank of the United States,[110] & other disputable matters. He annoyed me wofully, for I was sleepy and he had nothing to say worth keeping awake to hear, and after getting from him all the useful information about the country that he possessed, I let him talk on and went to my dreams, his garrulity notwithstanding. His companion was a modest well behaved & very handsome man who had walked to Fort Mitchell from the Chattahoochie river, where he had been just able to save his life. The steamboat, Van Buren, on which he had been a passenger having caught fire in the night, when loaded with cotton and burnt to the waters edge. He seemed impressed with a deep sense of the danger he had run, and was enormously more

110. The second Bank of the United States was the subject of heated political controversy at this time. In 1832 President Jackson had vetoed a bill to recharter the bank and in 1833 had begun to withdraw government funds from the bank; opponents feared that the lack of a central banking system would lead to financial chaos. See Robert V. Remini, *Andrew Jackson and the Bank War*, (New York, 1967); and Bray Hammond, *Banks and Politics in America from the Revolution to the Civil War*, (Princeton, 1957).

annoyed than I was with the inconsequential babbling of the man
along side of him. This last, I believe, for I was asleep, [a] great
part of the time continued to prate until the sound of his voice was
drowned by the rolling of the wheels across the wooden Bridge of
the Chattahoochie at Columbus.

At one oclock we crossed the river and reached Columbus. This
is a large and thriving town in Georgia at the Falls of the
Chattahoochie, which empties into the Appalachicola, and through
that finds its way to the Gulf of Mexico. The Bridge across it at
Columbus is built of wood, on stone piers, and is after Town's
plan.[111] Steam boats ply regularly up to the town and the rich and
improving country in the neighbourhood well adapted to the
culture of cotton, furnishes them with ample employment. Now
there are difficulties about the title to the land where the town of
Appalachicola is located on the Gulf which retards its increase.
When these difficulties are removed, and which is speedily
expected, Appalachicola will no doubt make rapid strides and
become a place of trade only second to the cities of New Orleans &
Mobile — for there is a back country to support it which is daily
increasing in wealth and population.

It was too late when we reached Columbus to get any thing to
eat at the Tavern. To pass away the time and overcome the
cravings of my appetite I determined to shave, and put on clean
linen. This after some difficulty I accomplished, and felt more
refreshed than I had anticipated, even. In some of my memoranda
of former journeys I have I think pronounced an eulogium up[on]
clean shirts and a smooth chin for a traveller. Experience confirms
what I then said. I was a happy man this evening. I even felt like
going over to the Tavern opposite and praying admission to a
ballroom, from which the sound of music and the tread of merry
feet came across the square of the town to the cold and comfortless
apartment in which I had performed my ablutions.

We got rid of our talker at Columbus, and our shipwrecked friend
left us: but their places were filled by gentlemen who were bound
Northwardly. At three oclock in the morning of the 11th
December we left Columbus. I went to sleep forthwith
notwithstanding the wind & rain which came in certain holes in

111. A lattice-pattern truss for long-span bridge construction, developed in 1820 by Ithiel
Town, later of the prominent New York architectural firm of Town & Davis. Town built a
number of bridges in the South between 1818 and 1825, aided by his aggressive promotion
(Harvie P. Jones, *Bulletin* of the Association for Preservation Technology, 1983, XV:3, 39).

the curtain next me, and did not wake until we stopped at Phillips to breakfast. After a tolerable meal, and a very unnecessary delay on the part of the driver we got under way again between 9 and 10 o'clock. The rain had ceased by this time, so we put up the curtains of the stage and had a view of a rich, well timbered and rolling country through which numbers of newly erected buildings were to be seen, and the fields of which showed all the marks of recent clearing and cultivation. This part of Georgia promises well and is by far the most interesting of any of the country I have travelled through, since leaving Mobile. Georgia is not a nullifying state. No! Nor would Carolina be one did her cotton crop equal that of her southern neighbour.[112]

We are in luck for wedding parties. This morning we received a gentleman & lady who are on their way to one. Our good breakfast, the sudden clearing of the sky, the fine country made us inclined, this time, to good fellowship — the lady was mischievous and merry and after a ride of an hour we regretted that they had to leave us.

Eleven oclock brought us to Talbotton, quite a pretty village and deriving its chief importance from being the "county seat." We remained here only long enough to change horses and have the mail bag looked into and then resumed our journey to Macon. We dined very indifferently at a changing house — crossed the Flint river in a flat boat at sundown — got an excellent supper in the small & pleasant village of Knoxville, and drove into the large and rapidly improving town of Macon on the Ockmulgee river at about midnight. Steam boats ascend the Ockmulgee to Macon, and a handsome wooden bridge on stone piers spans the river at this place. Macon is only six or seven years old and promises to become a place of very considerable importance. It is admirably situated in a cotton growing district and has an excellent water communication with Darien on the Atlantic seaboard. We did not remain here long.

A tedious and uninteresting ride through a country inferior in appearance to that which we passed through yesterday brought us to

---

112. In 1832 South Carolina asserted a constitutional right to "nullify" or declare null and void federal law, in this case a tariff act. The following year President Jackson threatened to use force against the "Nullifiers." Although the state yielded to the power of the national government, the theory of nullification persisted in South Carolina and throughout the South. See William W. Freehling, *Prelude to Civil War: Nullification Controversy in South Carolina,* (New York, 1966).

Milledgeville[113] the Capital of the state of Georgia by eleven
oclock. The situation of this place is most unpicturesque. The
commissioners, so I was told who were appointed to travel about
and select a site for the Capital grew tired as they approached this
spot, and finding a spring of pure water under the shade of some
large trees sat down at it and made a comfortable meal. They arose
in such good humour with the situation, that they determined to
look no further, but identifying the spring and the clump of trees
ordained that here should through further generation, assemble the
legislative wisdom of Georgia. And so it is. While other sites more
favorable to capitals but not so well suited to a comfortable
lunching place on a hot summers day are to be found within the
circuit of a few miles from Milledgeville, — this one has been
adopted, and a small town, looking like all towns that depend
solely upon the presence of the State or county government for
support, has been built to flourish in busy activity during the winter
and rest in utter idleness when the Legislature is not in session.

The statehouse in Milledgeville is a large building in the Gothic
style, built of bricks and stuccoed.[114] Its appearance is very
imposing and its general exterior proportions good. The stage did
not remain long enough for me to get a look into the interior.
There is a penitentiary here also — presenting nothing remarkable
in the appearance of it from the high[way] which passes close under
its walls. I'm sure I should dislike to be in the penitentiary any
where, but I think I would prefer any other place, even the District
of Columbia to Milledgeville.

Hitherto we had been travelling in a six passenger coach. We
were now put into one built for four passengers with a seat
subsequently squeezed into the middle, and seven persons were
packed into it. After trying to sit on the hind seat with two others
I found it utterly impossible and got into the middle of the middle
seat. I now annoyed the man behind me by sitting on his knees,
dear knows, unwillingly enough for he was a thin lath of a fellow
and I had become so sore by long riding in the stage that I desired
no unnecessary friction upon certain parts of me. He took it into
his head that I put him purposely to inconvenience, and poked me
most abominably with his bony patella where I could least abide it,
and we quarrelled outright. He was the Elder of my negro traders —
and very deaf — and in the conduct of our dispute I had to bellow

113. Capital of Georgia from 1804 to 1867.
114. Completed in 1833. The building burned in 1894 and was rebuilt. In 1941 it burned
a second time and was again rebuilt (Frederick D. Nichols, *The Architecture of Georgia*,
Savannah, 1976, 64).

to him which made the whole contention a subject of great mirth to the others in the stage. He told me that one or other of us must leave the stage — to which I replied I was very well agreed, and did not care how soon he vacated his seat. He fumed & swore — but by keeping my temper I got the other passengers on my side and really think that if he had not been quiet he would have been left on the road side. This was the only quarrel I ever had in my long and numerous journeys — and here I happened to fall in with a peevish devil who was too deaf to listen to reason, and too contemptible to get angry with. We crossed the Oconee in a flat boat.

We stopped at Sparta at about 8 oclock and got an excellent meal. It is a pretty village well situated. Warrenton another village of the same size with Sparta we reached at mid night, and while the usual delay for fresh horses and the mail took place, we got something to eat and stretched our cramped and aching limbs — for truly I never was in such a purgatory as this infernal stage coach made for me.

The three passengers who caused this squeeze were a member of the Legislature returning home to Savannah by way of Augusta and two gamblers — black legs[115] — both the latter well behaved and quiet and the member of the Legislature well informed and polite. The latter and myself had Colonization over between us, and I explained to him the Maryland plan.[116] He seemed delighted with it and thought it would remove all objections to Colonization in the South, if it could be carried into effect throughout the country. I dont know when I ever met with a gentleman of more liberal views than this one. I only regret that I did not learn his name before we parted at Augusta.

After breakfasting soon after sunrise we were hurried into the stage — for there was a doubt whether the mail would not be lost, that is arrive too late — and driven at a rapid rate through a flat uninteresting country to Augusta which we reached at 10 o'clock.

Augusta is situated on the bank of the Savannah river here a broad and handsome stream navigable for steam boats. The streets are very wide, and the houses well built, and there seemed to be all

115. Swindler, especially at cards or races.
116. The Maryland Colonization Society differed from the national group on such matters as emancipation and the conduct of the settlement of Liberia. In 1834 it set up its own colony, Maryland in Liberia, at Cape Palmas (Staudenraus, 233). Latrobe frequently spoke on the issue of colonization; several pamphlets, derived from his speeches, were later published, including *African Colonization,* (Washington, 1862).

the bustle and business of a thriving town going forward while I remained there — a precious short time to be sure but long enough, from 10 till twelve oclock to take a walk for a mite up and down the main streets. There were cotton wagons in great numbers, the oxen very quietly lying down, their yokes forcing them to put their heads together like wise judges posed by some astounding position of a limb of the law, — and standing along side of the team a negro waved to and fro a seven or ten foot goad, and gossipped with all comers. The market house is in the center of the business avenue of the town, and has quite an imposing appearance. There are many worse looking places in the world than Augusta, I assure you.

I had intended proceeding by the Hamburgh and Charleston rail road to take steam at Charleston for Norfolk, but upon reaching Augusta, the weather was so fine, and promised to continue favorable for traveling for some days & the moonlight nights were so bright, — and then there was a chance of bad weather in the steam boat at sea — that I changed my mind and determined to stick to the mail and see the huge leathern bag that I had accompanied all the way from New Orleans safe in Petersburg Va at all events. So at 12 oclock I got into a nine passenger coach converted into a six passenger one by taking out the middle seat — so that we had as much room as we wanted and to spare, a most agreable contrast to the travelling purgatory in which I had been stowed away for the last twenty hours. Our company was five in number. Colonel Whitner,[117] a gentleman in the service of South Carolina as a civil engineer, my two negro dealers and a deaf german with big whiskers and a ready laughter at whatever was said of a merry or serious kind — he grinned at all alike. We crossed the Savannah upon an uncovered wooden bridge, built high to be out of the way of the freshets and, turning to the left proceeded along a street on one side of which was the river and on the other a long row of low common looking frame buildings with china trees planted before them, and around the doors of which were clusters of negroes of both sexes and of all ages: This was the negro market, where the dealers kept their slaves, and to which the planters on both sides of the river resorted to make their purchases. I forbear remark as you know my opinion upon this subject. After remaining for a few minutes at the Hamburg post office, where my negro dealer wanted to make some enquiries about the ownership of the

117. Possibly Joseph N. Whitner, who lived near Greenville, South Carolina.

slaves along the bank of the Savannah already mentioned, we continued our journey. We crossed the rail road and commenced the ascent of quite a long and steep hill from the summit of which there was a lovely prospect across the Valley of the Savannah with Hamburg and Augusta giving life and vivacity to the foreground of the landscape. Small time was allowed for us to look — our coachee cracked his whip and away flew his four splendid horses down a long narrow road among trees of all kinds whose branches almost met overhead. The rail road continued in sight for many miles, now raised upon piles across a lower portion of the country, now constructed in an excavation but for the most part coinciding very nearly with the surface of the ground. Seven miles from Augusta we stopped to dine at a snug house by the road side, enlivened by the close neighbourhood of one of the saw mills with which the country hereabouts abounds and which was ripping away at huge trunks of pine trees and converting them into rail road string pieces for the Northern market. The dinner was a very good one, and the girl that waited on us a perfect beauty with the smallest hands I ever saw for her size, — quite of the dimension aristocratic. Upon resuming our seats in the stage we continued, generally in sight of the rail road to Aikenville[118] where there is an inclined plane worked by a stationary engine and where a village has grown up within the last year. I saw two engines waiting for the arrival of the train from Charleston with their steam flying off in whizzing jets from the safety valves while a dense body of black smoke rolled from their chimneys as the resinous pine wood used for fuel was thrown upon the fire. The engines looked old and ill kept — and were apparently almost on their last legs. The name of the maker was Stevenson Liverpool[119] — so said the brass plate over the fire door. At Aikenville we changed horses and at four oclock left the place and pursuing a more northerly course lost sight of the railroad altogether. The roads continued very good and we rode pleasantly enough along. The sun went down — the twilight passed quickly — the shadows of the trees grew strong on the ground, as the moon assumed the ascendancy in the unclouded sky, and nine oclock came upon us much sooner than I had hoped for. We had become tired of talking and fastening the curtains down

118. Now Aiken, South Carolina.

119. Possibly refers to Robert Stephenson & Co., early builders of railroad steam engines, including those for the Liverpool and Manchester Railway. George Stephenson, the father, founded the first locomotive workshop in 1823 (Gustav Reader, *The World of Steam Locomotives*, New York, 1974, 26-46).

tight all round and drawing up the blinds had composed ourselves
to sleep — occasionally rousing up to ask the driver the usual
question, "how far to the changing house." We were in the forest
all the time and the huge pines rose high above our heads. I had
questioned the driver, and received his reply that we were three
miles from the next stopping place, and had fixed myself
comfortably to continue the nap in which I had been for the last
hour. One of my negro dealers was squirmed up in the bottom of
the stage — leaving two of the rest of us on each of the seats. I had
scarcely found a soft place for my head on the pillow of Mrs.
Gilliat's comfort, before a violent jolt of the stage threw the four
benchers upon the sleeper on the floor & roused all hands. "Brisk
rate we're going" said I. "Quite so," replied Col. Whitner. I let
down the blind enough to see and thought that we did indeed fly
along through the woods at great speed. Faster and faster, the trees
appeared and vanished and I began to think we had a very Phaeton
of a fellow on the box. Finally we made a most uncomfortable lurch
to one side, and then a corresponding one on the other — and
then the stage seemed to be going madly ahead. I began to suspect
that all was not right now and said — "We are run away with I
fear." "I have been thinking so for the last minute or two"
answered Col. W. — quite calmly — "but keep still dont move
gentlemen." There appeared at this instant to be a diminution in
the speed of the stage, and the youngest negro dealer cried out
"Nows your time driver, stop them now. Nows your turn to hold
in." "I doubt whether we have a driver" said I and putting my head
out of the window I saw in truth that his box was vacant and that
our horses were going at frantic speed along a straight but very
narrow road with trees closing in upon both sides of us — and as
they dashed through the wood I saw their shoes as their heels were
thrown up and the moonbeams glittered momentarily upon the
iron. "Sit still gentlemen," said Col W — in a calm grave voice.
"We are in the hands of a merciful providence. We will soon, if He
wills it, be at the changing house and the horses will no doubt stop
at the stable. Sit still he said more demurely as the man on the
floor seemed inclined to rise up. Sit still or we are all dead men."
And we did sit still — and there is nothing in the world that calls
for more courage than to be able to do so in such a situation. —
We did sit still while the four splendid animals urged their way with
undiminished velocity. We did sit still. But all of life to be
remembered came up to the heart and almost stifled it — Years

were crowded into seconds. Home, friends, life death, this world, eternity — Oh how many thoughts filled the mind during the few brief minutes of that whirling ride.

I looked out for the others from time to time, and at last I saw the change house with lights streaming from its windows. And a hope of safety came — but it came only to be destroyed. The horses turned shortly round, and grazed the gate before the little tavern, then darted to their stable door opposite then turned again, then again, and hurried as fast as ever down a narrow lane in the forest, nearly parallel with the main road but running in the direction opposite to that by which we came. This diagram will show you how our course lay.

I had now remained still until the break on which I relied failed and the horses hurried past their usual stopping place along a narrow road with which they were unacquainted. I determined to make an effort for life, and quickly as I could calculated all my chances of success in what I proposed to do. I looked out of the window and seeing a clearing on my side ahead, I undid the cord of a large blue cloak I had on, and as we came opposite to it, rose and putting my head and body out of the window seized the iron railing on the top of the stage. I found the cord of the cloak still fast about my neck and the weight of the cloth holding me back. With one hand I loosened it again and in an instant was on top of the stage by a muscular effort that I only wonder at when I recollect. I immediately, after pulling my cloak, the cord of which was round one arm, across the roof went forward to see if the reins could be got at. They were on the ground, three on one side and one on the other of the stage. Nothing could be done here for the general safety so I hurried to the boot behind and laying down on it with my feet hanging towards the road, and just able to see the horses heads in the lead over the top. I held on to the edges of the leather on each side and determined to stick by the stage so long as I saw the horses keep the road. I had just got fixed here when the door flew open and one of the passengers in his shirt sleeves pitched into the road, and rolled over and over like a log. I gave him up for dead, for he was on the ground still when I lost sight of him. But my attention was now called to my own safety. We had got to the brow of a hill — a ravine was in the middle of the road — a considerable descent exaggerated by the deceptive light was before us and the time had come I thought to leave my position so sliding down till my feet touched the ground, I made the motions of running with the greatest rapidity and let go. I landed in perfect safety, and after thanking audibly the Almighty for my preservation, ran after the stage that was whirling down the hill before me. Before I reached the bottom, I saw two negroes coming out of the woods with dogs — from 'possum hunting — I sent one back with directions to stay by the man that had jumped out. I borrowed the hat of the other, and with him ran along the road. After passing the bridge at the bottom of the descent I met two of the passengers limping towards me to look after the man who had jumped out. I told them that he was with the negro by this time, and we all agreed to look after the stage and Col. W. We had not gone far before we came up to this last also limping — and soon after reached the stage fast locked with a saplin[g] — without leaders, and the wheel horses foaming and stamping as they were held by the breast chains only to the end of the pole. The elasticity of the sapling had prevented the stage being dashed to pieces which it would have been had it struck a solid tree. A house was hard by, and in a short time the leaders were caught — and the man who first threw himself out the elder negro dealer came hobbling up, sadly shaken, as were all the others, who had at different times followed his example. Col. W. & myself were not hurt at all. The rest remembered the event for many a day. Before long the driver from the changing house came up, and tackled up the harness so as to get the stage back. It may be supposed we did not ride back, but preferred the walk of two miles to being drawn by the devils from whom we had so narrow an escape. At the change house we found our driver who had been thrown off by the jolt that alarmed us and awoke us at first — much bruised but with whole bones.

Little supper was eaten, save by two of the passengers the elder negro dealer & the deaf laugher — who had been half scared to death in the stage and sick unto death almost as we were on our flight — but who eat as heartily as cassowarys[120] when the danger

120. Any of several large birds, related to the emu.

was over. I uncorked my bottle of wine and my companions & myself emptied it. I drank a tumbler full, and felt it no more than if it had been water. My account of this escape has been so lengthened, I will make no reflections. I never want to ride such another race, you may readily suppose.

We left the change house as soon as the stage could be prepared for we had lost time in our excursion to the Southward, and it required haste to save the mail, that is, to get it to Columbia, before the hour limited by the contractors agreement expired. As may be imagined we all continued wide awake; though for that matter we might have slept soundly, as the roads were good and without accident or alarm we drove into Columbia the Capital of South Carolina just as day began to dawn. We barely saved the mail — for we were nearly two hours past the usual time and had been given up. Before entering the town we crossed the Congaree river upon an excellent bridge. Columbia is a pretty and well built town, and the State house is an ancient and venerable building of wood. The Legislature are in session and the Unionists and the Nullifiers had just agreed to suspend further quarrelling about the act oath and "make friends," each party putting their own construction upon the obnoxious parts of it. The minority was too strong to be driven to desperation, and it was wisdom to be at peace. Another instance of the truth of the old saying that the better part of valour is discretion.

The sun was rising as we left Columbia. We had changed a part of our company. Col Whitner and the deaf Dutchman remained, and an Eastern merchant looking after some of his debtors was but an indifferent substitute for Col W. But he was good natured and talkative and that is a great deal in a stage coach companion for a journey that extends over 1200 miles.

Sunday, December.

We breakfasted at a clever little inn on the road side about eight oclock, and travelled on through an uninteresting country towards Camden. [121] We were now on revolutionary ground. The pine woods through which our route lay had in their time been filled with the partisan patriots of Marion and Sumter & Huger, and the green riders of Tarleton. [122] Rugely's mill lay a little to the left. The

---

121. Scene of British victory during the Revolutionary War, August 26, 1780.
122. British cavalry whose uniform had green facings, commanded by Sir Banastre Tarleton.

sandy highway was now as it had been in the times of 1780 & 81.
The Torys had camped here. The Whigs there — here [had] been a
skirmish — there a wild and daring feat of individual courage. The
country all around was crowded with materials for bold tales of
adventure. I got on the box — not to gaze at swelling hills and
broad meadows but to envy the old pines that had witnessed the
deeds of the bygone days of the revolution. It was Sunday — and it
spoke well for the emigrants to see their wagons under the trees
their horses unharnessed about them, and the families quietly seated
around, reading, talking, or dozing — but observing the day and its
decorums. And this was a sight that met my eyes constantly, for we
were now in the country from which a great portion of the
emigration takes place, and many were the reasons for the
abandonment of home which revealed themselves in the poor
barren fields which scarcely alternated with vast tracts of forest
land, where the pine had deterred the laborious husbandman from
attempting to make the soil productive in cotton or grain.

Towards noon we emerged from the woods, and the Country
became more open. Camden appeared some two or three miles
ahead, as we crossed the brow of a hill and looked across a broad
extent of low lands in the midst of which the Wateree wound its
tortuous way, a broad and sluggish stream now urged into unwonted
alacrity by recent rains. A wooden bridge on Towns principle has
once afforded the means of crossing it but a freshet had carried the
further abutment of wood down to the ocean, and we contented
ourselves with a good ferry boat that plied below it. The approach
to the bridge on the Camden side was lined with gigantic trees,
that seemed the survivors of the primeval forest, — which had
heard the shock of contending hosts — beneath whose shade
English and American had alternately rested, and whose picturesque
beauty made up for many a weary mile of barrenness of my journey
to them. On either side cotton fields extended far to the right and
left of fairer promise than any which I had seen since leaving
Georgia — and as we approached the town, the site of the battle
field so disastrous to the American arms was pointed out to me.
The former situation of Camden is now occupied by brickyards the
present town being built further to the North some hundreds of
yards.

We drove up to the Tavern amid a crowd of good Carolinians,
whom the idleness of the Sabbath collected round the door. As
soon as I got out, I started off to an old building which had been

pointed out to me by the driver as the headquarters of Cornwallis, when Cornwallis was. I hurried through the town and soon found myself in the fields and in front of the uninhabited mansion — a large two storied edifice of wood — a melancholy sight it was & I was almost as dull before it as no doubt were many of those some fifty years ago. And yet I felt something like enthusiasm and romance as I walked hither and thither on the deserted premises. Cornwallis — Rawdon — Tarleton. Their names sanctified the spot. DeKalb, Gates — Washington, Howard — Here had they all battled. What fools we are. I got back as soon as I could to dinner. The genius of the place haunted me however, and while my teeth were employed upon tough mutton my fancy was conjuring up recollections of the past; and when I asked of the innkeeper who dealt out slices of ham close by me, of the days of the Revolution, and found him as ignorant as though the cause of freedom had never been jeoparded where his roof tree now rose, I could scarce contain the expression of my contempt.

> My country! Every lovely spot
> Where war's dread 'larum rung in former days
> By tranquil river, or by mountain grot
> Lives in my memory, — never to be forgot, —
> A peopled world, — where fancy often strays
> Lee's Tarleton sweeping through the woody path
> Wild troopers at his heel
> Hears the dread shriek of misery or wrath
> As falls his steel.
> — *cetera desunt* —[123]

Nothing particular struck me in Camden, except the monument to DeKalb[124] the cornerstone of which was laid by Lafayette when he made his tour of triumph through the country — a plain, neat marble tomb — and a rare piece of sculpture over the entrance to the market house — a spread eagle — the most preposterous specimen of the art I ever beheld, and what kept me laughing before it all the time I was sketching it. To describe it were impossible.

123. *Trans.*: the rest is missing.
124. The DeKalb monument, a marble obelisk on a granite pedestal, stands in front of the Presbyterian Church in Camden. Both the church and the monument were designed by architect Robert Mills, a pupil of Benjamin Latrobe. See H. J. Pierce Gallagher, *Robert Mills, Architect of the Washington Monument, 1781-1855*, (New York, 1935).

Southern Travels

At Camden the Eastern merchant left us and in his place we got a Virginian who had been living for some years in Vicksburg Mississippi and was now on a visit to his friends near Petersburg. He was in a sorry plight. He had been, in Charleston to places where he ought not to have been, and had been robbed of his pocketbook by the fair associates of the house and was now pennyless — Not having money to pay his stage fare. The fare be it understood was not paid at starting but paid to the agent of the line, forty miles ahead, at Cheraw. In a little while he joined conversation with my negro dealers, and they soon discovered that they were all three Virginians from the same neighbourhood & had common acquaintances. It was then that he told his story, but without making any application for assistance. This however as they afterwards told me they afforded him to such extent as he desired. I pitied him much. He had learned a bitter lesson as to his company in large cities, and will not offend again I will venture to swear.

Our road lay through an uninteresting country over which we were wheeled with great rapidity — to my great annoyance, for my ride of the other evening has made me very nervous after night fall: and when I got into the stage after the second change I found that the driver stowed away his whips as unnecessary to hasten the speed of the four beautiful and strong horses that he was to drive. For ten miles the length of the route, I could hear him constantly coaxing his team, and well understood that he was afraid of them. Of course I slept but little. At midnight we stopped at the supper house, having been made to travel so far for our meal that an agent of the stages might have the profit of furnishing it. We were well supplied however and did not grumble more than was excusable in people who were cold sleepy and tired. I shaved myself here — a matter fit to be noted in the memorabilia of my journey — for the opportunities of doing so were rare I assure you. Two hours more brought us to Cheraw on the Pedee.[125] Here we paid our fare; and leaving the village, for it is nothing else, — and but a poor one to boot, crossed the River on a Bridge of wood, and soon after found ourselves in North Carolina.

Nothing to be seen but woods, where pines predominated and occasional cotton fields.

December 15th.

Breakfasted this morning at the house of a colored person, who

125. Pee Dee River.

also to the duties of Tavern keeper joined those of stage coach man. To save the law which required that the mail should be in charge of a free white person — a little white boy road [rode] along with him on the box. Our negro driver was a clever merry soul, and I rode with him outside the greater part of the day. He told me monstrous stories of alligators & varments. After sundown we found ourselves descending from a table land, and in the broad valley before us saw the town of Fayetteville, which we soon after entered in time for an excellent supper. This place was nearly destroyed by fire a few years since, the traces of which are still visible in solitary and blackened stacks of chimneys scattered here and there among blocks of new and handsome dwellings. Fayetteville I was told has prospered much since the conflagration, and exports by the Cape Fear river, which is within a mile of the town large quantities of cotton annually. the rail road by wh. this is conveyed from the town to the landing is constructed altogether of wood with a round topped rail, — the car wheel is cast to fit. It is found to answer

only indifferently well, and as may be readily imagined from the marginal sketch. The friction is very great.

    We left Fayetteville in good spirits — having had a good supper. Our Virginia friend remained there, and in his stead we took in a raw Yankee who had "a notion" to turn cotton planter and had come to look out for land. At midnight we stopped to change horses at a modest looking house on the wayside, where an old lady had prepared coffee — and better coffee and a neater supper, I never had anywhere, — The house was the most comfortable too that I had been in, out of the towns, since I left New Orleans. I forget her name. It deserves a more durable record than these pages.

    Towards daylight we took in a very pretty country girl the sister of the driver who amused me much by the conversation which she had with the Yankee — and soon after sunrise we drove into Raleigh the Capital of North Carolina. The State house[126] here was destroyed by fire some years ago — which would have been a

126. The original brick statehouse, designed by Rhodam Atkins, stood from 1795 to 1831, when it burned. The present statehouse on the same site was designed by New York architects Town and Davis and erected between 1833 and 1840.

matter of but little regret, had it not involved the destruction also of Canova's statue of Washington which was in the center of the building. They are now engaged in putting up a building of granite which will be fully equal to the Legislative Halls of any other state in the Union. The material is excellent and the design beautiful. It is said that the statue can be restored. I much doubt it. Peeping through the enclosure of logs that has been raised for its protection from the rubbish of the walls rising around I saw very little to remind me of the well known engraving. The idea of the statue is bad, and I have heard it said that Canova[127] was by no means satisfied with his work — Washington was in the costume of a Roman — barelegged — among the pines of Carolina. I should like to have heard the remarks of the first legislature that assembled after it was put up. They must have required volumes of explanation to understand it. Most probably however, they fancied that the scantiness of clothing proceeded from the poverty of the people during the Revolution, and that such garments as the general had were cut after the fashion of that day. Chantreys statue of Washington in Boston[128] is excellent in costume, but the attitude in certain positions makes you think that he is about pitching a quoit — and has folded his cloak around him to get it out of the way — Causici's Statue in Baltimore[129] is a good conception, and is free from the objection to Chantrey's, the subject being the same; but the marble was of a 'scant pattern' — the right side of the figure is a right line when seen from the front — But this is nothing to my journey —

[End of journal]

127. Antonio Canova, Italian sculptor, commissioned in 1815 by the state of North Carolina to execute a statue of George Washington. Canova used a bust by his contemporary Ceracci as a model for the head. The statue was completed in 1821 but did not arrive in this country until 1824. After the fire, the ruins of the statue were placed in the State Hall of History. In 1908 the Italian government, using the original model from the Canova Museum at Possagno, presented the state with a plaster replica (Frances Davis Whittemore, *George Washington in Sculpture*, Boston, 1933, 34-35, 38-39). The remnants that Latrobe saw are now stored in a warehouse of the North Carolina Museum of History (Information courtesy of Raymond L. Beck, curator, North Carolina State Capitol, May 6, 1986).

128. Sir Francis Chantrey, English sculptor whose statue of Washington, in the main hall of the State House at Boston, was unveiled in October 1827 (Whittemore, 45).

129. Henrico Causici, Italian sculptor, whose statue of Washington was erected in 1829 on top of a marble shaft in Baltimore (Whittemore, 83). The statue "represents Washington at the instant when he resigned his commission (after the revolution) into the hands from which he had received it" (John H. B. Latrobe, *Picture of Baltimore*, Baltimore, 1832, 183).

INDEX

Stanton Frazar, Director
Patricia Brady Schmit, Director of Publications
Louise C. Hoffman, Publications Assistant
Editorial staff:
Lynn D. Adams
Joan L. Sowell
Jan White, Head of Photography

The body of this book has been set on a Mergenthaler Linotron
202W in Goudy Old Style, designed in the early 1900s by Frederic
W. Goudy. Goudy, a midwestern accountant, became one of the
most prolific type designers in the history of the printed word.

Jacket design, book design, and hand-drawn titles: Michael Ledet,
    Word Picture Productions, New Orleans, Louisiana
Typography and production: Devlin/Wenger Associates, New
    Orleans, Louisiana
Color separations: ProGraphics, Clearwater, Florida
Printing and casebinding: Rose Printing Co., Tallahassee, Florida